Dr. Joel R. Beeke
2115 Romence N.E.
Grand Rapids, MI 49503
616-459-6565
Fax 459-7709

HALLELUJAH!

Hallelujah!

Christian Worship
Herbert M. Carson

EP ——————————————— EVANGELICAL PRESS

EVANGELICAL PRESS
16/18 High Street, Welwyn, Hertfordshire AL6 9EQ, England.

© Evangelical Press 1980
First published 1980

ISBN 0 85234 142 3

Bible quotations are from the New International Version

Typeset in Great Britain by Solo Typesetting, Maidstone, Kent
Printed in U.S.A.

Contents

Introduction

Worship is the declaration by a creature of the greatness of his Creator. It is the glad affirmation by the forgiven sinner of the mercy of his Redeemer. It is the united testimony of an adoring congregation to the perfection of their common Lord. It is the summit of the service of the angels and the climax of the eternal purpose of God for His people. It is man's supreme goal here and the consummation of his life in heaven.

If, then, worship is the ultimate aim of Christian living, we need to learn as much as we possibly can about this great theme. If life here is a preparation for life hereafter, then our worship here is a prelude to the adoration of heaven, and we must prepare with the concentration of all our powers. If to worship God is to realize the purpose for which God created us, then we must give ourselves wholeheartedly to this service.

Thank God we are not left wondering how we should worship. We are not like the Athenians with their shrine to an unknown God, for the living God has spoken. He has made Himself known. He has declared the fulness of His character and it is this which elicits the response of the worshipper. He has told us how we are to approach Him, and what kind of worship is acceptable to Him. The how, the why, the when, the where — all these questions have been answered by the living God. He has spoken clearly on these matters, and left the abiding record of His revelation in the Bible.

Nor has He simply given us a book and left us to draw our own conclusions. He has given His Spirit to dwell among His people, and indeed to live within each one of them, so that each congregation is the temple of the Spirit, and the body of each Christian is also His temple. But the Spirit who dwells within the worshipping temple of the people of God is the Spirit who moved men to write the Scriptures and who enlightens our minds to grasp their truth.

The Holy Spirit has thus given us the pattern for worship in the Bible. He helps us to understand the principles of biblical worship, and He so stirs us that our growing understanding evokes from the depths of our souls the response of adoration, praise and thanksgiving. So we begin our study of the subject of worship where indeed we must begin every other study — with God's revelation in His own Word.

1 The Old Testament background

The basic ideas

The God of the Old Testament is not simply one among the multitude of deities in the ancient world. He is not a tribal god on the same level as the Baals of Canaan or Ishtar of Babylon. He is the Lord of lords, the God of the nations, the God of history, the Lord God Almighty. All that God says and does flows from this basic truth that God is the Sovereign; He does not wait on man, for the initiative is always His. He is not dependent on man, for He is sufficient in Himself, and it is His condescension that He even allows man to approach Him. He is the infinite eternal God before whom the appropriate attitude is summed up in Samuel's prayer: 'Speak, Lord, for your servant is listening.'

Thus it is God who declares both the obligation of man to worship his Creator, and the way in which he should come. Hence the call to worship is a firm command: 'Fear the Lord your God, serve him only' (Deut. 6:13). This command is backed by the reminder that the Lord is a jealous God. Like the husband or wife who cannot tolerate any rival within the intimate relationship of marriage, so the Lord brooks no divided loyalty. Allegiance to Him must be total.

These absolute demands of the sovereign God are seen in the stipulations for the worship of the tabernacle. In all the detailed description of the construction of the tabernacle and its furnishings, in all the specific regulations for the worship to be offered there, we meet a recurring emphasis on the final authority for all that is done. Moses receives clear instructions as to the work: 'See that you make them according to the pattern shown you on the mountain' (Exod. 25:40). So, again and again, as the work proceeds, it is noted that all was done 'as the Lord commanded Moses'.

This insistence on God's sovereign prerogative in determining the pattern of worship is reflected in the tragic history of King Uzziah. The early days of his reign were marked by great achievements. But, instead of being humbled by the goodness of God, the king became inflated with pride. In spite of the clearly declared will of the Lord that only the divinely ordained priests should enter the temple, Uzziah transgressed the limits which God had set. The resistance of the priests proved to be the echo of God's censure. The sentence of judgement which left Uzziah a leper till the day of his death was a solemn reminder to Judah that the Lord will not tolerate any deviation from His mandate.

The sovereignty of God and the submission of the worshipper are reflected in the actual Hebrew words used to describe worship. There is in the first place *abodah,* that is, the service rendered by the *ebed* or slave. But slavery then was not like employment today which depends for its continuance on the goodwill both of employer and employee. The slave belonged to his master and was committed to serve him. He was available at any time, and was entirely subject to his master's wishes. He could not dictate, he must obey.

There is, however, a qualification to be made. The ideal slave was not one compelled by his condition to serve reluctantly, but the willing servant. This is seen in the regulations for the release of slaves after six years' service. A slave might of his own free-will forego his release. He might reply to the offer of liberty, 'I love my master....I do not want to go free.' Then followed the ceremonial ratification of the new relationship by the master. 'He shall take him to the door or the door-post and pierce his ear with an awl. Then he will be his servant for life' (Exod. 21:6).

Handley Moule captured this Old Testament picture of glad and total commitment in his hymn:

> My Master, lead me to Thy door,
> Pierce this now willing ear once more:
> Thy bonds are freedom; let me stay
> With Thee, to toil, endure, obey.

When the translators in Alexandria in the second century B.C. produced the Greek version of the Old Testament, the Septuagint, they rendered *abodah* by two Greek words which were later to be employed in the New Testament. One of these is *latreia* (though the corresponding verb *latreuo* is more frequently used). In ordinary Greek usage it was applied to any service rendered, as for example the service of a mother to her child. So in Romans 12:1 it is used to sum up the response to the call to 'offer your bodies as living sacrifices, holy and pleasing to God'. Such a total self-offering is spiritual worship.

The other Septuagint word which is used in the New Testament is *leitourgia* which is reflected in the English word 'liturgy'. The word was not, however, confined to the religious sphere for it had its secular usage in the service rendered by the citizen to the state. So it is used in Philippians 2:30 for the service the Philippians wished to render to Paul. Its religious usage is seen in Acts 13:2 where the corresponding verb *leitourgeo* is employed: 'while they were worshipping the Lord'. Such worship was the liturgy or service rendered by the servants to their heavenly Master.

Another Hebrew word which reflects this attitude of the worshipping servant of the Lord is *shachah,* which means 'to bow down'. Thus Abraham's servant 'bowed down to the ground before the Lord' (Gen. 24:52). So, too, when the glory of the Lord filled the newly dedicated temple of Solomon all the Israelites 'bowed down with their faces to the earth on the pavement and worshipped and gave thanks to the Lord' (2 Chron. 7:3 R.S.V.). The Septuagint word, in this case, is not used by the New Testament writers. However, as we shall see later, they emphasize the same attitude when they speak of 'bending the knee'.

At the very heart of biblical worship is this attitude of humble submission and reverence. There are other elements such as praise and thanksgiving and, at times, exuberant joy. But always there is the underlying attitude of awe and humility. The worshipper may come with confidence to God. He may present his needs with the assurance that the Lord hears. But he is always the obedient servant before his Master, with his spirit bowed in adoring submission before the Lord of hosts.

The Old Testament emphasizes the holiness of 'the high and lofty One . . . he who lives for ever, whose name is holy' (Isa. 57:15). As a consequence there is a firm stress on the need for atonement. Before a man may approach God, he needs to be reconciled to the One whom he has offended by his sin. Hence the whole structure of Old Testament worship is rooted in the sacrificial system. Before a man brings his burnt offerings, which speak vividly of his total commitment to God; before he brings his peace offerings, with the emphasis on fellowship with his Lord; before he joins in the praise of the temple — he needs the forgiveness purchased by the sin offering. This last-named sacrifice brought into focus the ugliness of sin in the sight of God, the demands of divine justice that sin should be punished, and the merciful provision of the sacrificial victim as the substitute to bear the penalty. It was all a foreshadowing of the coming of the Messiah who would offer the final and sufficient sacrifice, on the basis of which rebel sinners might be reconciled and worship and adore their pardoning God.

Closely allied to this emphasis on the need for repentance and forgiveness as the basis of worship is a firm assertion of its inward character. The natural man, when he thinks in religious terms, inevitably construes the demands of worship in a formal and external way. So he thinks of particular ritual acts which have to be performed, particular holy days which must be observed, particular forms of prayer which should be used. Against this empty externalism the prophets constantly mount a vigorous protest, as they insist that true worship, which is acceptable to God, is inward. Jeremiah indignantly repudiates the complacency of the formalist who deludes himself by the frequent use of the phrase 'the temple of the Lord' as if the repetition of a religious formula could cover up a total spiritual lack. Similarly, Micah asks his searching question: 'With what shall I come before the Lord and bow down before the exalted God?' His reply, prompted by the Spirit of God, is incisive: 'He has showed you, O man, what is good. And what does the Lord require of you? To act justly and to love mercy and to walk humbly with your God' (Micah 6:6,8).

Closely linked to this stress on the inwardness of true worship is the prophetic insistence on the need for a corresponding consistency of life. It was only when David had been driven out of his refuge of lies to humble himself in repentance that he not only learned the thrill of pardon, but overflowed in delighted praise of God (see Psalms 32 and 51).

Amos, the rugged prophet of Israel, castigates those who bring their sacrifices and yet at the same time are blatantly unrighteous in their lives: 'I hate, I despise your religious feasts; I cannot stand your assemblies. Even though you bring me burnt offerings and grain offerings, I will not accept them . . . But let justice roll on like a river, righteousness like a never-failing stream' (Amos 5:21-24). His great contemporary in the southern kingdom echoes his call to righteousness: 'On the day of your fasting, you do as you please and exploit all your workers. Your fasting ends in quarrelling and strife. . . . Is this the kind of fast I have chosen, only a day for a man to humble himself? Is it only for bowing one's head like a reed and for lying in sackcloth and ashes? . . . Is not this the kind of fasting I have chosen: to loose the chains of injustice . . . to share your food with the hungry . . . when you see the naked, to clothe him?' (Isa. 58:3-7.) It all recalls the psalmist: 'If I had cherished sin in my heart, the Lord would not have listened' (Ps. 66:18).

The feasts

Turning to the characteristics of Old Testament worship, we discover the prominence of the great annual festivals. Three times in the year Israel was to celebrate the feasts. First came the Feast of Unleavened Bread culminating in the Passover; then the Feast of Weeks celebrating the first-fruits of the harvest and, finally, the Feast of Ingathering or Tabernacles at the close of the harvest season. These annual gatherings were intended to remind Israel of fundamental tenets concerning God's relationship with His people and so to stir them to grateful praise. They were to recall God's deliverance at the first Passover season, and celebrate the redemption which had set them free. They were to acknowledge at each new harvest-time the constancy of the Lord who was faithful to His promise that seedtime and harvest would not fail. They were to end the year, not only with praise for harvest, but with the ceremonial erecting of booths, which would remind them of God's care for His wandering people in the wilderness. It was all a stimulus to faith that the Redeemer would still provide for His pilgrim people until the end.

Five days before the joyful harvest thanksgiving of the Feast of Tabernacles came the most solemn day of the year —

the Day of Atonement, *Yom Kippur*. It was a day for self-examination, for repentance and for confession. It was the day when the two goats were taken, when one was slaughtered as the sacrificial substitute and the other, over whom the high priest had confessed the sins of the people, was led away into a desert place. In the solemn ceremonies of the day much of the Old Testament teaching on worship is vividly portrayed. The sinner dare not approach God because the wrath of God reacts against all ungodliness and unrighteousness. Only in the divinely appointed way may he approach. His mediator is the high priest; his reconciling agent is the sacrifice, and his goal is joyful fellowship with God, in which he will be able to praise his Creator for all His mercies.

Praise is not, however, tied to festival times. Indeed one notable feature of Old Testament worship is the prominence of praise. We hear Moses and the Israelites singing their song of victory after their deliverance from Egypt (Exod. 15). We see Jehoshaphat leading his army against the Moabites with a song of praise on their lips (2 Chron. 20:22). We listen to the trumpets of the priests and the cymbals of the Levites as they praise the Lord at the laying of the foundation of the restored temple (Ezra 3:10). We glimpse Isaiah's vision of the ransomed of the Lord returning from exile with songs as they go back to Zion (Isa. 35:10). Above all we hear the swelling tide of praise which wells up throughout the Psalms and reaches its glorious crescendo in the final psalm. Here all the musical instruments are employed to accompany the people of God in a final outburst of exultant song.

The temple

Closely allied to the spirit of praise is the intense delight which the worshippers obviously found in the temple worship. It is superbly expressed in Psalm 84: 'How lovely is your dwelling-place, O Lord Almighty! My soul yearns, even faints for the courts of the Lord; my heart and my flesh cry out for the living God . . . . Better is one day in your courts than a thousand elsewhere; I would rather be a doorkeeper in the house of my God than dwell in the tents of the wicked.' It is because the temple is the place where God manifests His glory that the psalmist responds with great delight of soul.

It is all an anticipation of the New Testament fulfilment in the temple of the Holy Spirit. There, without the magnificence of Solomon's architecture, the humblest company of believers exhibits the surpassing glory of the presence of the indwelling Lord. There, too, God makes Himself known and the Christian finds his deepest delight in the communion of saints, and in fellowship with them he praises God. Indeed one might say that the temple worship of the Old Testament, with its music and song, is not only an anticipation of the praising churches of the New Testament, but of the heavenly choir joining in the final hallelujah chorus of the redeemed in glory. The great cloud of witnesses is now in heaven singing the praises of the Lamb, but they learnt the basic theme of the heavenly song during those years when God was preparing Israel for the great days which were to come when the Messiah would at last appear.

Temple worship exercised a profound and abiding influence on the worship of the New Testament churches. This was only to be expected, for that worship had not been the product of Israelite religious theorists, but had been revealed by God. It is understandable therefore that there is a direct line of spiritual descent from the temple in Jerusalem to the temple of the Spirit established in every local congregation of believers. The latter were the heirs of the lessons which God had taught their spiritual ancestors. The characteristics of temple worship which we have already seen thus continued in the basic pattern of Christian worship.

Shorn of the temple's external pomp, its robes, its incense and its ceremonial, New Testament worship maintained the same fundamental principles. The sense of awe and reverence are still present, and inevitably so, for the God of majesty, whose thunders were heard at Sinai and whose glory filled the temple, is still declared in the New Testament as 'the holy Father' and 'the consuming fire'. The intimacy of the psalmist's appreciation of God as the Father who pities His children, continues in an even more inward fashion in the adoring cry by the adopted child, 'Abba, Father', and in the assurance of the Lord's prayer. The joy, which constantly erupts into song in the temple, surges to even greater heights in Peter's description of 'an inexpressible and glorious joy' (1 Peter 1:8), and finds expression in the 'psalms, hymns and spiritual songs' of the Ephesian church. The sense of history highlighted by the observance of the great Jewish festivals continues in the Christian recollection of the decisive historical events of the birth, death, burial and resurrection of the Saviour.

But with all the continuity there is also a deep contrast. The Old Testament was the period of preparation, the New Testament that of consummation. The promises gave way to realization, the prophecies to fulfilment, the types and shadows to the substance. So the whole structure of the ceremonial law and the external pattern of temple worship were replaced by the simplicity of worship in the church. The sacerdotal ministry, with the priestly hierarchy reaching its apex in the mediating high priest, found its fulfilment in the Messianic High Priest who has offered the final sacrifice and has now constituted every believer as a priest, with the right of direct access into the presence of God. Sacerdotalism has given way to congregational worship.

It was a failure to see this radical new beginning in the New Testament that led to the grotesque perversion of worship which has been a major tragedy of Christian history. Whether it is the transformation of the simple services of the early church into the ornate and elaborate ritual of pontifical high mass, or the proliferation of every kind of liturgical ceremony — these alike testify to an abysmal failure to appreciate that the old order has passed and the new has come.

This dual theme of continuity and contrast is worked out in detail in the Epistle to the Hebrews. There is continuity, for the Christians who run the race are part of a great company, some of whose most distinguished members are listed in the Old Testament roll of honour recorded in chapter 11. But there is also marked contrast, for the old system of Levitical worship has been abrogated. The Levitical priests fulfilled their ministry by divine mandate, but always its temporary character was evident. They were mortal, so that each priest's ministry terminated in death, whereas Christ's is an everlasting and unchanging priesthood. They were themselves sinners, even in their ministry on behalf of fellow sinners, whereas Christ was 'holy, blameless, pure, set apart from sinners' (Heb. 7:26). Their sacrifices were symbolic, since they could only deal with ritual uncleanness, for the blood of bulls or goats could not cleanse sin (Heb. 10:4). His, however, was a perfect and unrepeatable sacrifice. The Levites opened the way into an earthly sanctuary, whereas Christ has gained access for His people into the presence of God.

For the people of God in the time of their infancy, as Paul puts it in Galatians (4:1 ff.), the picture language of the ceremonial law and the Levitical ritual was a means of spiritual blessing. But, with the coming of the Messiah and the out-pouring of the Holy Spirit at Pentecost, the people of God have come of age. To revert to the old forms is not only a sort of spiritual childishness; it is worse, for it ignores the funda-mental fact that the final revelation has been made, the final sacrifice offered and the new pattern firmly and finally estab-lished. There is no need, as the English Reformers expressed it in a typically vigorous way, 'to borrow gee-gaws out of Aaron's wardrobe'.

The abiding spiritual principles of temple worship are still the basic structure of Christian worship; but in its simplicity, its congregational character and its confident proclamation, the latter has parted company with ceremonialism and sacer-dotalism. The scaffolding of the old temple services was vital during the time of preparation for the coming of the Messiah. Now, however, the scaffolding has been removed to reveal the temple of the Holy Spirit. To try to erect it again is not only foolish, but tragically obscures the finality and perfection of the work of Christ.

The synagogue

The transition from the elaborate ritual of the Levitical ser-vice to the simple worship of the church of Christ was not so sudden as it might appear. To turn quickly in our Bible read-ing from Malachi to Matthew may obscure for us the fact that something like four centuries elapsed between the close of the Old Testament and the opening of the New. But while the voice of prophecy was silent during that period until John the Baptist sounded the old prophetic note, the provi-dence of God did not slumber. God was still at work among the Jews, preparing them for the coming of the Messiah and for the emergence of the new Israel. One important element in this providential ordering of the nation's life was the development of the synagogue which was to have such a powerful and direct influence on the order and worship of the Christian church.

It is difficult, if not impossible, to say when exactly the synagogue began to develop, but its roots probably go back to the time of the exile in Babylon. With the destruction of the temple in Jerusalem and the scattering of the nation, centralized worship, with the daily services and the religious festivals, became impossible. Localized centres inevitably developed to meet the spiritual needs of the exiles. The word 'synagogue' is a Greek term meaning simply 'a place of assembly'. Then it became the technical designation of a Jewish place of worship. In the following centuries the dispersion of the Jews continued until there were colonies all around the Mediterranean. Even though the temple had been restored in Jerusalem after the return from Babylon, the spiritual needs of the exiles still remained. These needs were met in the development of the synagogues which served each of the scattered communities.

In the simplicity both of its furnishing and of its form of service, the synagogue was markedly different from the temple and was clearly, in the providence of God, a preparation for the developments which were to come with the advent of the Messiah. There was no altar, since sacrifices were not offered. Instead there was a portable ark containing the scrolls of the Law and the Prophets which were read from a platform. The place of the sacrificial offerings was taken by the reading of the Law — the *Torah* — and the recital of the prayers.

The *Mishna*, the Jewish oral law which dates from the second century B.C., outlines the five parts of synagogue worship. It began with the *Shema* — from the Hebrew word 'to hear'. This was a repetition of the call of Deuteronomy 6:4: 'Hear, O Israel: The Lord our God, the Lord is one.' Along with the reading of Deuteronomy 6:4-9, the *Shema* embraced Deuteronomy 11:13-21, with its promises of blessings to an obedient people, and Numbers 15:37-41, with its insistent call to obedience.

After the *Shema* came the readings, first from the Law and then from the Prophets. This was followed by an exposition and an exhortation to the congregation to apply the Scriptures. A visitor who was qualified might be invited to expound. So Jesus read from the prophecy of Isaiah in the synagogue at Nazareth and then expounded the Word (Luke 4:16). Nor was this an isolated occurrence, for Matthew speaks of His going throughout Galilee 'teaching in their synagogues, preaching the good news of the kingdom' (Matt. 4:23). In the same way Paul was invited by the rulers of the synagogue at Pisidian Antioch: 'If you have a message of encouragement for the people, please speak' (Acts 13:15).

After the preaching came the benediction which ended the service. The singing of psalms was probably interspersed throughout the service, and the early church continued to follow this custom of psalm singing. Indeed the whole structure of the synagogue service was reflected in the emerging pattern of Christian worship where prayer, praise, the reading of the Scriptures and the preaching constitute the essential elements. The similarity is accentuated if we compare the role of the elders or rulers of the synagogue, of whom one was the preaching elder, with the elders who are described in the Pastoral Epistles, and who combined a teaching and also a ruling function — hence their other title of bishop or overseer. The synagogue was indeed God's providential preparation for the church.

2 The New Testament pattern

The new situation

The early Christians who appear in the opening chapters of
the Acts were Jewish and still maintained their close links
with the temple and the synagogue. Peter and John clearly
saw it as a normal thing that they should go to the temple for
prayer (Acts 3:1), and Paul found it quite acceptable to visit
Jerusalem for the ceremonies of Pentecost in order to discharge his Nazarite vow (Acts 21:17-26). The synagogue, as
we have seen, was Paul's priority in visiting any new town.
Yet at the same time there were further factors at work. The
increasing opposition of the Jewish leaders and the storm of
persecution which broke over the church not only drove the
Christians from Jerusalem, but increasingly alienated them
from the meeting-places of Judaism.

The influx of Gentile believers accentuated this trend since,
being uncircumcised, they would have had no place in the
temple. Indeed it was the mistaken notion that Paul had introduced a Gentile into the temple area which produced the riot
recorded in Acts 21. The fall of Jerusalem and the total
destruction of the temple in A.D. 70 were thus, in the providence of God, the final stage in a process of demarcation
between the new Christianity and the old Judaism which had
already become a reality.

There was, however, an even more significant factor contributing to the emergence of a new pattern of worship, which
was clearly the lineal descendant of the Old Testament, but
was yet quite distinctly new. This new factor was the outpouring of the Holy Spirit at Pentecost, with the subsequent completion of the revelation of God, as the apostles spoke the
final word to complete what the Old Testament writers had
begun.

The day of the new covenant foretold by Jeremiah had

now come. The Messiah had accomplished His ministry, offered the final sacrifice which abrogated all lesser sacrifices, and was now exalted as the one all-sufficient High Priest. As a result the doors were opened, not only to Jews, but also to Gentiles. The gospel age had dawned and new principles were needed for the men and women of this new age. They were principles embodying the ageless truths inherited from the prophets, but also declaring the new life in the Spirit which is the hallmark of New Testament Christianity.

This present chapter is in a sense introductory to the remainder of the book. It will attempt no more than a general survey of the essential character of New Testament worship. The chapters which follow will be the detailed outworking and application of the general principles described here. There is, however, a great value in such an overall picture. In examining details it is easy to fail to see the wood for the trees. Close study is clearly necessary, and in some controversial areas may require meticulous attention to details. At the same time it is profitable to stand back and see the total pattern.

As we do so it is important to keep in mind that the presentation is not one of idealized figures engaged in some spiritual activity, the whole created by the fertile imagination of the writer. We are looking rather at actual men and women of flesh and blood, with all their foibles, weaknesses, fears, problems and sins, who are yet rejoicing in the corporate worship of God Almighty. We are also being summoned by the Holy Spirit to a like consecration.

The governing principle is still the same as in the Old Testament, in that the Word of God is the standard by which every practice is to be assessed. Paul warned the Colossians against 'self-imposed worship' (Col. 2:23), which Calvin well interpreted as 'self-invented'. The apostolic precepts and prohibitions are the guiding lines which must be followed, with positive teaching on the one side and warnings of erroneous deviations on the other.

The aim also remains the same, and inevitably so, for the glory of God is always the goal towards which the life of believers is directed. Indeed the vision of the glory of the Lord is to be the guiding principle not only when they gather together for worship but in every area of their lives. The basic aim of the services on the Lord's Day is not the blessing of the congregation — though clearly that is prominently in view — but the glory of God. This means that our primary questions will not be directed to the breed of psychological advisers in the realm of influencing congregational responses — if indeed they should ever be made in that direction! The consideration rather which will dominate the minds of those who prepare for the service of worship will be that in every aspect God will be magnified.

Order, freedom and simplicity

Closely allied to this concern with the glory of God is the principle that 'everything should be done in a fitting and orderly way' (1 Cor. 14:40). The God of creation is the God of order, not chaos. The God of providence is the God who directs the details both of historical events and of each individual life to the ultimate end of realizing His purposes. So order and reverence will characterize the services. 'God,' says Paul, 'is not a God of disorder but of peace' (1 Cor. 14:33).

It is, however, an order which is quite compatible with freedom. The Lord who established an order in the balance of nature did not put the skylarks He created in cages. So the orderly pattern of worship is not to be a prescription for a liturgical strait-jacket which represses the freedom of the people of God to express their praise. Indeed, it was because of this very freedom that Paul had a problem on his hands at Corinth, where freedom had been made an excuse for licence. His answer was not to lay down a rigid liturgy which would have controlled such excesses, but to encourage a continuing freedom while stressing decency and order as the moderating influences.

With the glory of God as the primary aim, there is also in the New Testament the clear recognition of the needs of the worshippers. Three times in 1 Corinthians 14 Paul insists that the edification of the church is a basic concern. Whether he is controlling the excesses in the exercise of tongues, or directing the Corinthians in the pattern of a truly congregational worship, he keeps reminding them that, 'All . . . must be done for the strengthening of the church' (1 Cor. 14:26).

Since, however, the church is not normally composed exclusively of either mature theologians or immature converts, the aim of those who lead the worship will be to meet the varied needs of young and old, of recent converts and of long-established believers. These worshippers have come with all their varied needs — as forgiven sinners who are deeply aware of sinful failure, as struggling believers with problems or fears or sorrows, as those full of gratitude for some signal deliverance recently enjoyed, as those with a burden of concern for unconverted or backsliding relatives. All of them are to be in view as the service of worship is directed towards edifying the whole congregation.

Linked to this aim of edification is an insistence on intelligibility. The congregation must understand what is happening and must be able to participate. It was this principle of intelligibility which led to Paul's command that the gift of tongues must not be exercised in public without an interpreter, and in any case must be strictly limited. For the same reason he declared prophecy to be of greater value in that an intelligible message is brought, to which the church can respond. How can they respond, he asks, how can they say an intelligent 'Amen' at the giving of thanks if they do not know what the speaker has said?

A consequence of this emphasis on intelligibility is a stress on simplicity. Here is the point where the contrast with the temple worship of the Old Testament is seen at its most marked. The elaborate ceremonial, the ornate vestments, the incense and the lights — all have given way to an essential simplicity in which a pastor in the ordinary dress of his congregation conducts a service where the surroundings are secondary, the ceremonial absent and a simple approach in prayer and praise and preaching is the pattern.

The Lord's Day

A notable divergence from the Old Testament is the precise day for the weekly gatherings for worship. The seventh day gives way to the first as the sabbath sees the emergence of the Lord's Day. There is no specific command anywhere in the New Testament that the change should be made. It is this silence which is one of the main arguments of the Seventh Day Adventists who continue the observance of the sabbath. If in fact the sabbath and the Lord's Day are identical then clearly they have a strong case. There are, however, other explanations for the change of day.

In the first place there is evidence in the New Testament that the change of day has already taken place. Paul's instructions about the collection refer to the money being set aside on 'the first day of the week' (1 Cor. 16:2). When he visited Troas, the first day was clearly the time for the breaking of bread and also the occasion for sustained preaching. It was not as if he had only a day or so at Troas, thus necessitating the observance of the Lord's supper on the most convenient day, for in fact he was there for seven days, and the first day of the week was obviously the normal day for the Lord's supper.

The same pattern is seen in some of the early Christian writings. The *Didache* which dates from around 100 A.D. gives instructions: 'And on the Lord's day of the Lord come together and break bread and give thanks, having first confessed your transgressions' (14:1). Later in the century Justin Martyr, who died in 163 A.D., wrote in his *Apology:* 'Sunday is the day on which we all hold our common assembly, because it is the first day on which God, when he changed the darkness and matter, made the world; and Jesus Christ our Saviour on the same day rose from the dead; for on the day before, that of Saturn, he was crucified; and on the day after it, which is Sunday, he appeared to his apostles and disciples' *(Apology* c.67.8).

There is also a difference of emphasis. Paul lists the sabbath among those things which 'are a shadow of the things that were to come; the reality, however, is found in Christ' (Col. 2:17). It was part of the prophetic preparation for the coming of the Saviour, and the detailed sabbath regulations were like the detailed ceremonies of the temple, the picture language which anticipated the coming day. The same truth is developed in Hebrews. There the rest of the sabbath, when God rested from His labours, is seen as a type foreshadowing the gospel doctrine of justification by faith, when a sinner rests from his labours and relies upon the sufficiency of Christ. It is also an anticipation of the goal towards which his justification points when the believer enjoys the sabbath rest of heaven (Heb. 4:1-11).

As the churches became predominantly Gentile, a very different world was their context. In the Jewish theocracy, when the people of God lived within their own ordered society, the sabbath regulations could be carried out in detail. But now Christians were in a Gentile society where there was no sabbath rest. Very many of them were slaves with no control over when they worked. It is not surprising therefore to find that the service on the Lord's Day at Troas was held near midnight and that Pliny's letter to the emperor about 110 A.D. describes the Christians gathering for worship before daybreak. As many of them would have a long day of toil the pre-dawn or late night services were essential. But, as we have seen, the change of significance in the day was not simply an adaptation to a new condition of things. It was rooted rather in the conviction given by the Holy Spirit that the shadows had given way to the substance. The heart of that substance was the resurrection of Christ. Hence the Lord's Day became the festival which ousted all other festivals and which served as a weekly reminder that Christ had risen from the dead.

Prayer and praise

The church of the New Testament is a praying church. Christians were taught to pray as individuals and when they met together, prayer was a spontaneous exercise. Indeed it would be a false distinction to imagine that the prayer of the individual and the corporate prayer of the congregation are separate activities. It is noticeable that when Jesus taught His disciples to pray He put on their lips the title 'Our Father'. Every time the Christian prays, even though he is completely on his own, he knows himself to be a member of the body of Christ. He cannot isolate himself to engage in some act of individualistic piety. Always he is one with the people of God, and as he lifts his heart in prayer and praise he senses the nearness of a great congregation.

There is a fascinating picture of the church at prayer in Acts 4. It is an illustration of how a congregation should pray and, more than that, it is a call to prayer. It therefore will repay careful study though only some salient features can be noted here. In the first place it was a spontaneous reaction to the situation. They were facing a rising tide of hostility. What were they to do? The modern tendency would be to convene a meeting to discuss tactics, or perhaps to appoint a sub-committee to formulate ideas. Their reaction was an immediate and spontaneous one. They prayed!

The praying was audible. They 'raised their voices'. It was no inaudible mutter, nor a long-drawn-out and crippling silence such as blights some church prayer meetings. They could be heard, and doubtless they were quite uninhibited in the volume of sound they registered! Like children clamouring at home for attention because of some urgent need, so the children of the kingdom are encouraged in the New Testament to approach God with boldness as they make their needs known to Him.

There was also unity. They were 'together' not simply in the fact of physical nearness to each other, but in the sense of having a common concern and a shared confidence in the God to whom they came. The importance of unity is strongly pressed in the New Testament. So Paul urges the Ephesians: 'Make every effort to keep the unity of the Spirit through the bond of peace' (Eph. 4:3). It was after all when they were all together, united in obedience to the Lord's command, that heaven was rent and the Holy Spirit fell upon them. A like experience came to the believers in the prayer meeting of Acts 4 as those who had already lived through Pentecost were again 'filled with the Holy Spirit'.

With all their boldness, there is still a spirit of reverence. 'Sovereign Lord,' they begin, as they acknowledge the majesty and authority of their God. They recognize the truth expounded in Hebrews 4 that, while we may come with boldness in prayer, we must never forget that the God to whom we come is the King on the throne. Boldness must never degenerate into cheap familiarity, but must always come hand in hand with awe and godly fear.

A further important feature, and it is a typically biblical one, is their appeal to Scripture. So they quote the psalm before God, and make the Word of God the basis of their appeal. If God has spoken then He means what He says and will not fail to fulfil His promises. The reading of the Bible is thus not a separate activity from that of prayer. The two are interrelated in that the truths gleaned from the Word are intended to stimulate God's people to pray, and also to furnish them with a solid basis for confidence as they sue God to fulfil the promises. He has in grace committed Himself to these promises and their accomplishment He has pledged His own character to perform.

It is only after they have, in a spirit of reverent adoration, reflected on the glory and goodness of God that they turn to the actual needs of their present situation. They have clearly learned the lesson of the Lord's prayer that petition does not come first in prayer, but follows after the worshipper has been taken up with God's name and God's will. Adoration in the New Testament precedes asking!

Nor are they concerned with their own danger. Personal considerations of comfort or security do not enter into their thinking. They are too concerned with the spread of the gospel to be unduly troubled with possibilities of imprisonment or death for themselves. Boldness to speak the Word of God is a matter of greater moment than personal safety. It is an attitude reflected elsewhere in the New Testament. Paul's request for prayer support is with a view to his opening his mouth boldly to declare the gospel (Eph. 6:19). So, too, he asks the Thessalonians to pray for him 'that the message of the Lord may spread rapidly' (2 Thess. 3:1). An inward-looking church will have little of that passionate concern to see the Word spread, but then such a congregation will know little of the depth of the prayer life of Acts 4!

One of the Reformation confessions, the Thirty-Nine Articles, defines the visible church as 'a congregation of faithful men in which the pure word of God is preached and the sacraments be duly ministered'. Here are not only the basic elements of the church, but here also are some of the key features of New Testament worship. The church is 'a congregation of faithful men'; it is a company of believers. That is why, as we have already seen, the church is a praying people. They have come to know God as their Father, and in that knowledge they have learned, as children adopted into the family circle of heaven, how to say from their hearts, 'Abba, Father'.

In this worshipping congregation the preaching of the Word is of cardinal importance. There is a sense in which it is not simply one element but the very basis of the worship. It is through the preaching of the Word that the people of God will grow in their knowledge of God. It is through that growth that they will mature in their understanding of prayer. It is as they appreciate more and more the wonder of God's grace that they will be increasingly filled with praise. It is in the preaching of the Word that they will find the true meaning of baptism and the Lord's supper opened up, and will also hear the warnings against the erroneous ideas which pervert the message of these ordinances. Later in this book these issues will be treated in much greater depth.

Praise permeates the worship of the New Testament churches. How could it be otherwise? These men and women knew themselves to be the object of the amazing grace of God. To them the word 'redemption' was alive with meaning for they had been delivered from the slavery of sin. As they faced bitter persecution so they looked forward to the final triumph of the Lord, and to their own bliss in the glory of heaven. So, as the persecution waxed hotter, the songs rose more triumphantly. The theme of praise will also receive much fuller treatment later in this book, but in this general survey it is important to notice how prominent it was. It was the very context of their life; it was the delighted response of their hearts. It is no wonder that the great Old Testament word 'Hallelujah' lies at the heart of truly biblical worship.

Participation

The New Testament churches are seen then as worshipping congregations of believers. Drawn out of the world by the regenerating power of the Spirit they have been baptized into the body of Christ. They have not only found God as their gracious Saviour; they have also discovered each other as sharers together in the grace and mercy of the Lord. So they feel that their gatherings have been convened by the Holy Spirit. They find it a marvellous privilege that, sinners though they are, they may approach God. As they listen to the preaching of the Word, as they pray and praise together, and as they break bread, they know the enjoyment of the communion of saints. Nor are they mere spectators gathered to view a performance. They are themselves participants. They listen to the preaching, not with a passive acquiescence, but with an active and discerning concentration. They share in praise and prayer and ordinances as fellow members in the body of Christ.

The Greek word for fellowship *koinonia* (together with its allied words, the noun *koinonos* and the verb *koinoneo*) is of frequent occurrence in the New Testament. The basic element in the words is the root *koinos* or 'common'. Fellowship means 'having things in common'. To have fellowship is to share together in common experiences and common blessings. So Christians share in the grace of God (Phil. 1:7), in Christ (Heb. 3:14), in the Holy Spirit (Heb. 6:4), in the divine nature (2 Peter 1:4) and in the coming glory (1 Peter 5:1). They have a common salvation (Jude 3), a common faith (Titus 1:4) and a common hope (Eph. 4:4). They belong together — indeed the very evidence of their new birth is their mutual love (John 13:34; 1 John 3:14).

This basic unity determines the pattern of their worship. They do not come together as a number of individuals with particular needs and particular responses, but as a fellowship sharing together in the blessings of the gospel, and in a shared response to a gracious God. It is true that they come with their personal needs, but these are the needs of family members who want to share them with others, to pray about them with others, and with others to praise God. It is not surprising therefore that the glimpses we have of worshipping congregations in the New Testament are of active participants. Gathering for worship is never a mere assembly of individual Christians; nor is the service simply a passive enjoyment in the company of others, much as a group of like-minded people might appreciate going to a lecture together or enjoying a concert as part of a wider audience. There is naturally the fulfilment which comes in any human activity shared with others; but fellowship in Christian worship goes much further than this for it involves active participation.

In contemporary forms of congregational life, all of which claim to have their roots in the New Testament, there are strangely contrasting patterns. There are churches where one man virtually monopolizes the entire time apart from the singing of hymns and the Amen, which itself can often be rather perfunctory. At the other extreme is the neglect of a strong preaching ministry but freedom for anyone to take part. The one-man ministry on the one side, and the everyman ministry on the other, are alike divergences from what we find in the Acts of the Apostles and the Epistles. Here it is not a case of one or the other, but of both, with a clear preaching and also an active participation.

This participation is reflected in Paul's instructions to the

church at Corinth. Admittedly he is aiming to curb the chaos
which an unbalanced liberty had produced, but he still envisages an active sharing. So he describes what he sees as a
typical meeting: 'When you come together, everyone has a
hymn, or a word of instruction, a revelation, a tongue or an
interpretation' (1 Cor. 14:26). The same pattern is reflected
in his letter to the Ephesians where the mutual instruction is
given through the 'psalms, hymns and spiritual songs' (Eph.
5:19). This is not a prescription for an uncontrolled exercise
in individualism! Paul makes it very clear that there must be
firm control, and judging by his strong emphasis in the
Pastoral Epistles, this would be administered by the elders.
At the same time there was sustained preaching. So, when they
gathered at Troas for the breaking of the bread, and when
presumably they had the freedom to participate which Paul
describes in 1 Corinthians 14, there was also a sermon — and
a very long one at that, with rather disastrous consequences
for one sleepy member of the congregation!

If we turn to the very early days of the church in Jerusalem
we find these two aspects of preaching and participation.
Here also we may discover a clue towards ensuring the balance
between the two. The congregation was very large. Admittedly
many of the three thousand converts on the Day of Pentecost
may have been visiting pilgrims, but their departure home
would be more than offset by the daily influx of converts, so
that before long the number of men who believed had reached
five thousand (Acts 4:4). This large congregation gathered in
the temple courts where clearly there was preaching: 'The
apostles were teaching . . . and proclaiming in Jesus the resurrection of the dead' (Acts 4:2). It is hard to see how believers
who did not have the vocal power to reach a large congregation could share by any personal testimony or contribution
of praise or exhortation. But the large congregational assembly
was only one part of their corporate worship. So Luke makes
repeated reference to the house meetings which were clearly
a vital aspect of the church's life: 'Every day they continued
to meet together in the temple courts. They broke bread in
their homes' (Acts 2:46). 'Day after day, in the temple courts
and from house to house, they [the apostles] never stopped
teaching and proclaiming the good news that Jesus is the
Christ' (Acts 5:42). In such smaller gatherings there was

obviously the opportunity of sharing together in praise and testimony.

Where the local church is still at the stage where it can be contained within someone's house, then obviously active participation can still be a reality even when the whole church is assembled. When, however, a congregation has outgrown such premises and perhaps has grown very large numerically, there must be provision for the smaller gatherings if this vital New Testament element of participation is to be preserved. This does not mean that the large congregation should be reduced to a monologue. It is inconceivable that the crowds of converts in Jerusalem, whose interest had first been roused on the Day of Pentecost by the loud praise of the Spirit-filled believers, would themselves be so inhibited that the temple courts would not also ring with their praise. Nor is it conceivable that those same converts who had responded openly to the first preaching of Peter by asking the question: 'Brothers what shall we do?' would later lapse into a numbed silence which would preclude even an interjected 'Amen' or 'Hallelujah!'

Later, in considering the Lord's supper, we shall see that the note of sharing is central in that service. One might say that the emphasis on fellowship which lies at the heart of New Testament Christianity is focused in the communion of God's people at His table. But while the table should provide an opportunity for open sharing in praise and prayer and testimony, it is not the only occasion for such. We need such a movement of the Spirit as transformed men and women in the Acts into praising, sharing and obedient churches. Such participation is not manufactured by men. The man who employs the right psychological techniques, or knows how to utilize music, may well manipulate a congregation into what looks like spiritual participation. Such an induced expression of human emotions is, however, far removed from the worship of the Acts. There, men and women shared together in hearing the Word, in praise and prayer and breaking of bread, because the Spirit of God had baptized them into the body of Christ.

3 The trinitarian structure

Christianity was the child of Judaism and inherited the fundamental faith of Israel that there is only one true and living God. This basic conviction was not easily established in Israel. From the day when the Lord revealed Himself to Moses as the sovereign Lord — 'I am that I am' — the history of Israel was one of struggle between the worship of Jehovah and idolatry. Again and again they capitulated to the heathen religions around them, in spite of the urgent appeals of the prophets. With a like regularity they came under the judgement of God of which the prophets had given such stern warnings.

The judgement of God reached its climax in the great disaster of the eighth century when Judah was taken into exile to Babylon, leaving behind the smoking ruins both of the city and of the temple. Jeremiah's words, so long unheeded, had been fulfilled in grim detail. But one thing the exile did for the Jews was to root out the idolatry which had been endemic in their national life. True, they would lapse into legalism and materialism, and would finally reject the Messiah. But in spite of their spiritual blindness one truth was etched deeply upon their consciousness: 'The Lord our God is one Lord.'

With this background of firm monotheism it was all the more extraordinary that the disciples, with their Jewish upbringing, came to accord to Jesus of Nazareth divine honour. The claims He made were capable of no other interpretation than that He was God incarnate. Indeed it was for that reason that the Jewish leaders planned His death. Their accusation was clear. He was guilty in their view of blasphemy because though 'a mere man' he claimed 'to be God'. Yet His disciples accepted His claim, and their acceptance was repeated by that most implacable foe of the believers, Saul of Tarsus. It was the resurrection, the culmination of His authoritative ministry, His holy life and His powerful signs, which compelled them. Thomas's confession, wrung from him with great reluctance, sums up the response of men who felt they had no alternative explanation for this unique person: 'My Lord and my God.'

With the great event of Pentecost, and the powerful work of the Holy Spirit within individuals and within the church, further truth was revealed. The Spirit of whom Jesus had spoken in personal terms could not be viewed as an impersonal influence. It was not a case of the continuing impact of Jesus after His ascension. The Spirit had been promised as Jesus' own gift to His disciples, and as One who would take His place. His very title 'the Holy Spirit' declared His nature, for holiness in an absolute sense belongs to God alone. Peter recognized His deity in his confrontation with Ananias and Sapphira. The lies they had told were not simply directed to Peter but were, he said, an attempt to deceive the Holy Spirit; and this, in Peter's view, is the same as deceiving God.

It would be nearly three centuries before the doctrine of the Trinity was formulated in precise theological terms at Nicaea, but already in the New Testament the doctrine was declared. Every time a new believer was baptized in the name of the Father, the Son and the Holy Spirit, and every time the congregation was dismissed with the threefold benediction, there was an implicit acknowledgement of the deity of the Third Person of the Godhead. The church, while as firmly monotheistic as its Jewish ancestors, was, at the same time, committed to the richer truth that within the unity of the Godhead there were three Persons 'of one substance, power, and eternity'.

While doctrine is expressed in the creeds and theological statements of the church, it is also implicit both in worship and in practical living. To speak of worshipping God is at once to raise the question of the nature and character of the God we worship. Jesus' conditions for acceptable worship, that it should be 'in spirit and in truth', imply that we should worship the true God and do so in the way which He Himself has revealed to us. Thus, with the doctrine of the Trinity as our foundation, we should aim in the pattern of our worship to maintain both truths — that God is one and at the same time triune.

It is the self-disclosure of the one true God which moves us to worship in the first place. God has not kept silence. He does not dwell in some twilight region of uncertainty to which our only response can be speculation. He has revealed Himself in the marvels of the world He has created, in the moral law which He has set in each man's conscience, and supremely and finally in the person and work of His only begotten Son. Worship is the divinely prompted response of our hearts to all that God has made known to us about Himself. So the psalmist calls us to praise: 'Come, let us sing for joy to the Lord', and gives the reason why we should respond to his call: 'For the Lord is the great God, the great King above all gods' (Ps. 95:1-3).

God has made Himself known to us as the sovereign Creator. The Bible opens with an overwhelming disclosure of the creative power of the God who has called all things into being by His word. With an open Bible the Christian thinks of the creation around him and finds himself responding to the psalmist: 'The heavens declare the glory of God, the skies proclaim the work of his hands' (Ps. 19:1). To consider the vastness of the universe and to realize that it has come from the sovereign God and is kept in being by His power is to be moved to awe and wonder. This is the reaction which characterizes biblical religion, and which stands in marked contrast with the glib familiarity and flippancy so common in today's religious scene.

The awe which is produced by a glimpse of God's majesty is not, however, the only response. There is the further humbling realization that the Almighty One cares for creatures of the dust such as we are. Alongside the seemingly illimitable universe, our planet seems a mere particle and we ourselves less than specks of dust. Yet God has declared that He has made men in His image, and that He has given His Son to restore them to that image. To realize that God has made us, that He sustains us every moment, and above all that He has redeemed us — all this not only humbles us but moves us to praise.

Furthermore He is the everlasting God. He is not another creature of time. He is without beginning and without ending, the ever-present One, the unchanging One. To reflect on His eternity is to find our thoughts lifted from the level of the trivial and commonplace. To know such a God and to adore Him is to be raised from bondage to the pettiness and the perplexities which so often enslave us. We belong to One who knows the end as well as the beginning, and who is working out with a grand wisdom His everlasting purposes. So we take courage and as we bow in wonder and in humbled praise we rise to a new plane of confident trust.

He is the Holy One. He is 'the high and lofty One ... He who lives for ever, whose name is holy' (Isa. 57:15). His eyes are 'too pure to look on evil' (Hab. 1:13). Before Him the angels bow in wonder as they cry, 'Holy, holy, holy is the Lord of hosts.' Before Him also the congregation of His people bows. Unlike the angels we know the reality of sin. Even though we have known His grace in salvation we still know ourselves to be like the apostle Paul, who could only speak of himself as the chief of sinners. This blazing holiness humbles us, fills us with a solemn awareness of our own sinfulness, and so leads us to penitence. Confession of sin is thus a fundamental element in our worship and adds a serious undercurrent to all our praise. But it is not the solemnity of spiritual discouragement or despair. To know the depths of our sinfulness is to plumb the greater depths of His grace. To grieve in shame at our sinful selves is to rejoice with a fresh delight in the marvels of His pardoning love. Tears and smiles lie close together in Christian worship! It is a short step from the opening lines of Samuel Davies's great hymn of praise to its glad refrain. So we begin to sing:

> Great God of wonders, all Thy ways
> Are matchless, godlike and divine.

We reflect on our sinfulness:

> Crimes of such horror to forgive,
> Such guilty, daring worms to spare.

Then we continue in delighted adoration:

> Who is a pardoning God like Thee
> Or who has grace so rich and free?

This sovereign, omnipotent God, this One who is present in every place, and whose knowledge is all-embracing, this One who is holy and gracious, righteous and merciful – He is also the God of love. We live in this twentieth century where the currency of love has been debased, and what is called love is only lust with a humanistic veneer. But the love of God is utterly apart from human attitudes. Here there is no trace of the self-centred approach which is seen, for example, in the man who desires another's body only for the pleasure it gives to the possessor. Here rather is a love which is selfless, which gives and gives and gives again. Here is a love which will go to all lengths and face all pain in order to benefit the beloved. This is the love of our God. It is no wonder that a congregation is stirred as they hear such familiar words as, 'God so loved the world that he gave his only Son.' It is this theme which has stirred the preachers, the authors and the hymn writers of the Christian church to their highest pitch of eloquence, and to their supreme flights of poetry.

To reflect on the nature of the triune God is not only to be stirred to worship; it is also to discover the way in which we should come. One of the most succinct statements about our approach to God and one which is entirely trinitarian is Paul's word to the Ephesians (Eph. 2:18): 'Through him [Christ] we both have access to the Father by one Spirit.' Christ is the Mediator through whom we come to the Father, and it is the Holy Spirit who enlightens us to grasp the truths of God and enables us to receive them and apply them.

The Father — our Goal

It may seem obvious, yet in view of current practice it needs to be stressed, that the goal of our worship is the Father. There has developed a trend in which prayer is almost exclusively addressed to the Lord Jesus Christ — sometimes simply to 'Jesus'. It is almost as if the Father did not exist, or as if He were resident in some shadowy area outside our ken. When, however, we turn to the New Testament we find that the consistent pattern in prayer and praise is an approach to the Father. This is not to deny that there is a place for prayer and praise directed to the Lord Jesus. But in fact examples of this are very few. There is the dialogue between the risen Lord and Saul of Tarsus on the Damascus road, where clearly it is the Son of God who is involved. There are ascriptions of praise in 1 Timothy 1:12 and in the heavenly song of Revelation 5:8-14; 7:9-10. There seems to be no clear example of a petition directed to the Son.

By contrast, the normal pattern recurs again and again, where the Father is the object of praise and prayer. Jesus Himself established the pattern when, in teaching His disciples how to pray, He told them to say, 'Our Father'. When the believers in Jerusalem joined in the memorable prayer meeting of Acts 4:24, they addressed their prayer to the 'Sovereign Lord' that He would vindicate 'his holy servant Jesus'. For Paul the outcome of our adoption is that we pray with the kind of intimacy which an Aramaic-speaking child employed when he addressed his father as 'Abba'. It is not surprising therefore that in his great prayer for the Ephesians (Eph. 3:14) he kneels 'before the Father'.

The apostle Peter follows the same line. At the beginning of his first letter he praises God: 'Praise be to the God and Father of our Lord Jesus Christ' (1 Peter 1:3). The Epistle to the Hebrews is, if anything, even more emphatic. The high-priestly ministry of Jesus is extolled, and we are bidden to go to Him, but the ultimate goal is the throne where the Son brings us to the Father.

This emphasis on the place of the Father as the final goal in prayer in no sense derogates from the glory of the Lord Jesus Christ. His glory, after all, is that He has by His atoning death and triumphant resurrection and ascension purchased the right to act as the Mediator of His people. It is in discharging this mediating ministry, by bringing guilty sinners to His Father, that He displays His greatness and His glorious power.

Jesus Himself emphasized this very theme. He presented Himself as the door, as the light, as the way. Always it was to direct men to the Father: 'I am the way and the truth and the life. No-one comes to the Father except through me' (John 14:6). When He uttered what has been called His high-priestly prayer, recorded in John 17, He asked that the Father would glorify Him. But His aim was not simply that He should be seen in all the glory of His divine nature and of His redeeming work. He looked beyond Himself and so He prayed: 'Father, the time has come. Glorify your Son, that your Son may glorify you' (John 17:3).

The Son — our Mediator
Far from belittling the role of the Lord Jesus Christ, the trinitarian structure of biblical worship greatly enhances it. He is

the authorized Mediator of the Godhead. Indeed He is so exclusively the Mediator that it is only on the basis of His work that we dare approach the Father. To pray as we do in the name of Jesus is not simply to use a liturgical formula. It is to acknowledge that His name, revealing as it does His person and His work, is our only claim to being heard by God. So He tells us to come to God in His name (John 14:13; 15:16; 16:23 ff.). Paul echoes this in describing Jesus as the one Mediator (1 Tim. 2:5) and the Epistle to the Hebrews develops the theme in detail, as it contrasts the ephemeral glory of the Levitical priests with the surpassing and unchanging glory of Christ.

It is because of His mediatorial function that He must be central to all our worship. This means that the great truths about Him and His work will be the context of our worship. His eternal sonship, His incarnation, His atonement, His resurrection, His ascension, His second coming — these will be constant themes for our praise and the very foundation of our prayers. Worship will be focused on Him because He is seen in all the wonder of His advocacy in heaven. We magnify His name because He brings us to the Father's presence.

Such an exalted conception of Christ brings a sense of awe and wonder. Ambrose of Milan caught it in his great hymn, the *Te Deum:* 'Thou art the everlasting Son of the Father.' Charles Wesley has it in his familiar Christmas hymn:

> Veiled in flesh the Godhead see,
> Hail the incarnate Deity.

He touches in another hymn on the central mystery of the Incarnation, which is beyond the power of our puny understanding to grasp:

> Let earth and heaven combine,
> Angels and men agree,
> To praise in songs divine
> The incarnate Deity;
> Our God contracted to a span
> Incomprehensibly made man.

Awe in the presence of our Saviour is closely linked to praise. We marvel at His condescending grace. We bow in adoring wonder. We sing with Josiah Conder:

Worthy, O Lamb of God, art Thou
That every knee to Thee should bow.

Then we burst into praise, and the hymn writers furnish us with the great songs of the church of God. The former blaspheming slave-trader John Newton sets us singing: 'How sweet the name of Jesus sounds', and our hearts gladly reply. We sense the stirring of soul for an adequate means of expression as Charles Wesley prays, 'O for a thousand tongues to sing my great Redeemer's praise!' We are carried to a climax of praise with Isaac Watts:

Join all the glorious names
Of wisdom, love and power
That ever mortals knew
That angels ever bore:
All are too mean to speak His worth,
Too mean to set my Saviour forth.

This concentration on the glory of Christ, this magnifying of 'Jesus, the name high over all', leads to a deep confidence. It is for this reason that a time of worship can bring such comfort to a troubled or sorrowing believer. Here is the source of strength to face the conflict. Here is the undergirding to meet the buffetings of whatever storm may blow. Since Jesus has risen and since He is reigning we can sing with Newton, 'Begone unbelief, my Saviour is near.' We may rest as confidently as Toplady did on the unfailing grace of our Saviour:

My name from the palms of His hands
Eternity will not erase.
Impressed on His heart it remains
In marks of indelible grace.

Nor do we recall only His past triumphs, nor even His present heavenly reign. We are looking forward to His return. We are the pilgrim church on the road to the Celestial City. We are the church militant waiting for the final trumpet of God which will announce the return of our conquering Emmanuel and the overthrow of all His foes. Charles Wesley and John Cennick sweep us on from the opening line of their hymn on the second coming, 'Lo, he comes with clouds descending', until with a blend of exultant praise and joyful anticipation we cry,

Hallelujah! Come, Lord, come!

The Spirit — our Helper

Apart from the Spirit we could not even begin to worship. In our natural condition we are spiritually blind, so that even the glory of creation fails to show us the eternal power and Godhead of our Creator. We are deaf to the voice of God, and the music of heaven in the Scriptures makes no impression on us. The truths of the Bible unfolding the glory of the triune God are beyond our grasp. We are indeed, as Paul puts it, 'dead in transgressions and sins' (Eph. 2:1).

It is in this hopeless situation that the Spirit of God works. He begins to stir our dead souls as He imparts to us the life of God. He gives light to our understanding as He wakens us to the truths of God's Word. He speaks with a voice which penetrates our dull hearing and arouses us from our spiritual torpor. He probes our consciences and convicts us of our sins. He displays to us the glory of Christ as the only and all-sufficient Saviour. He moves our wills and enables us both to repent and to believe. He gives us assurance that in fact we have passed from death to life. He prompts us to pray (Rom. 8:26). He stirs us to praise (Eph. 5:13 ff.). He humbles us to adore.

The instrument which the Holy Spirit uses to accomplish His saving purposes in us is the Scriptures. They are His gift, for they came into being by His inspiring work: 'Men spoke from God as they were carried along by the Holy Spirit' (2 Peter 1:21). They are also the means He employs in awakening us and turning us to Christ. Peter reminds us of this: 'You have been born again, not of perishable seed, but of imperishable, through the living and enduring word of God' (1 Peter 1:23). This means that everything in our worship must be in accordance with Scripture. We are not to have recourse to modern psychological techniques to discover how to move people emotionally, and so to make them susceptible to the message we want to convey. We are not to relax people by some superficial display of religious entertainment, nor are we to quieten them by a soothing atmosphere when they need to be aroused. We are to be subject to the Scriptures in everything we do.

This means that our criterion for assessing the hymns we sing is not simply that poetically they are acceptable, nor that musically the melodies are appropriate. The supreme test is whether their themes conform to biblical truth. The great hymns are those which are subjective, in that they move our spirits, but they do so not simply by well-turned phrases, but by the truths which they express.

It is, however, not sufficient to have hymns which embody the great doctrines of Scripture. We must sing them under the direction of the Holy Spirit. It is possible to delude ourselves at this point. Greatly loved words can have a profound emotional impact, and the music can stir us deeply. But if the truths embodied in the poetry are to be the expression of true worship we must have the Spirit at work within us. As on Elijah's altar on Mount Carmel, the wood may be laid in order and the sacrifice ready for the offering, but the fire of heaven must fall. There is a vast difference between hearty congregational singing which can be induced by a crowd or by a good choir, and true praise which is elicited by the Spirit of God.

There is another biblical emphasis in the revelation concerning the Holy Spirit. It is the context in which He operates. It is true that He operates in the individual, dealing personally with each one of us — convicting us, renewing us, assuring us. But the wider context in which He delights to work is the congregation. The local church is 'the temple of the Holy Spirit' for it is there that He particularly makes Himself known. He is the Spirit of fellowship for He takes men and women of different backgrounds and with varied temperaments, and welds them together into the communion of saints. 'We were all baptized by one Spirit into one body' (1 Cor. 12:13). The unity we are to maintain is 'the unity of the Spirit' (Eph. 4:3). The love which should control the life of the church is 'the fruit of the Spirit' (Gal. 5:22). The readiness of the church to look out with missionary concern stems from the activity of the Spirit — it was He who intervened at Antioch to send Paul and Barnabas on their missionary journey (Acts 13:1 ff.). The gifts which the Spirit bestows in sovereign freedom are not merely for individual blessing but to enrich and build up the assembly (1 Cor. 12). The fruit of the Spirit (Gal. 5:22) which results in holy living is matured and developed within the fellowship, and is exercised in the mutual responsibilities of the local church, as a prelude to a wider influence.

The work of the Spirit in relation to the fellowship of believers must be viewed at three levels. There is the local situation where a company of believers are drawn by Him into church covenant. Then there is the wider sense as we reflect on the fellowship of churches stretching into many lands, and linking believers of many nations around the world. Finally, there is the church triumphant whose members have fought the good fight, finished the race, kept the faith and are now in the presence of Christ. These three aspects of the communion of saints will have a direct bearing on our worship.

When we gather in a local congregation we are to realize that we belong together. We are not simply a group of like-minded people who meet together in a similar fashion to members of some club or guild. We have been united by the life-giving power of the Holy Spirit to the body of Christ. As such we are not only in living union with the Head but in organic union with each other. A healthy body is one in which all the limbs function harmoniously under the direction of the brain. An injury to the nervous system can produce un-controlled spasms or varying degrees of paralysis. So the body of Christ is to function under the direction of Christ with the life of the Spirit reaching into each limb of His body. The frenzy of mere religious excitement, or the sluggish and moribund reactions of some congregations, are alike evidence of a lack of submission to the Head of the church, and to the direction of the Spirit.

In the worship of the local church, there will be a deep awareness that we belong to each other. This will be parti-cularly evident, as we shall see in greater detail later, when we meet at the Lord's table. But it should govern all our worship. After all, when the Lord taught His disciples to pray, 'Our Father', He did not give them some individualistic model of prayer. Every time they turned to God they were to remem-ber that they belonged to their fellow believers. The joys and sorrows of the members will thus be of common concern. The birth of a baby, the loss of a loved one, the marriage of a young couple, the loss of a job — all these and many other family concerns will be grist for prayer and praise.

The wider reference to the world-wide fellowship of the Spirit will be reflected both in prayer and praise. It is sadly possible for church prayer meetings, and for the intercessions at the Sunday services, to revolve around a narrow and parochial sphere. A church, however, which is aware of family links across the world will be keeping abreast of the changing international situation in order to be faithful in prayer to those who may be in testing circumstances in other lands.

The choice of hymns should also reflect this wider vision. We are not to be circumscribed by our own needs. We are not to lapse into a self-centred exercise in which the state of our own soul is the only topic for our songs of praise. We must constantly enlarge our horizon. We need to listen to the Lord's own commands: 'Lift up your eyes and look on the fields,' 'Go and make disciples of all nations.' With these themes as the context of prayer and praise, we will respond in spirit to the Old Hundredth: 'All people that on earth do dwell'. We shall sing with joyful and expectant faith:

> Jesus shall reign where'er the sun
> Doth his successive journeys run:
> His kingdom stretch from shore to shore,
> Till moons shall wax and wane no more.

There are further vistas still in our glimpse of the communion of saints. So we see ourselves gathered for worship as part of a greater company which praises God day and night in heaven. To be aware of our communion with those who have been taken from us by death is not to relapse into the erroneous practice of prayers for the departed. Apart from the total absence of such prayers from Scripture, and the firm emphasis on the present life as being finally decisive as to our eternal state, there is the further fact that believers in glory do not need our prayers. What could we pray for them? They do not need grace to face trial or disappointment or sorrow, for they have none of these. We do not need to pray for pardon for their backsliding or victory over temptation, for they are in a state of perfected holiness. They do not require our prayers that they might learn more of God's Word, for they are in His immediate presence 'lost in wonder, love and praise'.

This does not mean that we ignore the hidden company of heaven. Nor does it mean that we give a perfunctory nod of assent to the reality of their continued existence. Rather, they are a stimulus to us, for the great cloud of witnesses calls us to run with persistence the race set before us (Heb. 12:1 ff.). Hence the memory of those who have been parted from us for a little while is to prompt us to praise God for their lives, and to stir us to prayer that we might be likewise faithful in our generation. Isaac Watts's hymn revised by William Cameron strikingly presents the movement from a reflection on the present state of the departed Christians to overflowing praise. This vivid paraphrase of Revelation 7:9-17 opens with the exclamation: 'How bright those glorious spirits shine!' and moves through a consideration of their present joyful condition to a final burst of praise to the triune God who brought them to glory:

> To Father, Son, and Holy Ghost
> The God whom we adore,
> Be glory, as it was, is now
> And shall be evermore.

4 Our total response

'What is the most important commandment in the law?' This was the question put to Jesus by the spokesman of the Pharisees. Jesus' reply was to quote the word from Deuteronomy 6:5, heard so regularly both by Him and His questioners at the beginning of every synagogue service: 'Love the Lord your God with all your heart and with all your soul and with all your strength.' It is the requirement of God Almighty that His worshipping people give total and unqualified submission to His sovereign demands. To come to worship this great God is to come with an unreserved commitment. With every part of our being we aim to honour Him. With all our powers we purpose to ascribe to Him the praise which is His due.

To discuss the various elements in our total response must not lead us to imagine that this is a prescription for some kind of fragmented approach. We do not worship God, now with our mind, at another time with our feelings, at another with our wills. We are not a mere collection of various faculties and abilities. We are integrated persons, and all the diversity, physical, mental and emotional, blends together to produce the reactions and attitudes which are personally ours. Yet at the same time it is helpful to distinguish these various elements in our response since one or more may be neglected, while some may be overemphasized. To speak of 'heart and soul and strength' is not to refer to three different responses, but to speak of one person responding to God with all his various powers.

The intellectual response

All spiritual experience begins in the mind. The humanist notion of religion as 'morality tinged with emotion' is far removed from biblical religion, which is rooted in an intelligent grasp of the truth. This stems from two facts. In the first

place, God has made man in His own image. The account of
creation in Genesis 2 indicates that Adam was addressed as a
rational being, capable of naming the animal creation, and
able to appreciate the logical argument in which God presented the terms of blessing in response to Adam's obedience
and judgement in face of his disobedience. In the second place
God has revealed Himself in intelligible words. He has not left
men with some vaguely defined presence. The basic conviction of Scripture is that God has spoken in meaningful words.
His truth is propositional, that is to say, it is stated in sen-
tences which man, a thinking being, may grasp.

There is, however, a further factor in the situation. Man is
no longer in the condition described in Genesis 2. He is now
the fallen descendant of a disobedient Adam. But this Fall
has not only estranged him from God, it has profoundly
affected every part of his being. This means that his primary
faculty of thought has been darkened by sin. 'The god of this
age' wrote Paul (2 Cor. 4:4) 'has blinded the minds of un-
believers.' As a result man in his unregenerate state may be
highly intelligent and may reflect in his intellectual achievements the fact that the image of God, though sadly defaced,
has not been totally destroyed; yet such is the impairment of
his nature that he is only capable of understanding the gospel
as God by His grace gives him light in his mind. God has, in
Paul's words, made the Christian 'wise for salvation' (2 Tim.
3:15). As a result of his new birth and his renewal in the image
of God he is now capable of understanding the truths of God
which are 'spiritually discerned' (1 Cor. 2:14).

To worship God acceptably we must do so 'in spirit and in
truth'. There must be the communion of our spirit with God
in a living relationship of person to person. But if we are to
avoid the danger of self-deception, or of the idolatrous worship
of a projection of our own thoughts, or a figment of our own
imagination, we must ensure that we worship 'in truth'. It
must be the true God whom we adore, and our approach must
accord with the terms and conditions which He has Himself
laid down. Both the goal of our worship and the means of
achieving the goal are to be governed by the truth of God
which He has made known in the Scriptures.

This means that the context of our worship is the doctrinal
system of the Bible. Whether in preaching or praise or prayer,

every activity will be governed by the truths of the Bible. The first question to be asked is not whether some aspect of our worship is helpful or stimulating or enjoyable, but whether it is true. But to ask that basic question, we must have a criterion by which to judge. If we were to make our emotional response the only standard we would sink in a sea of subjectivism. Everyone would give his or her own individual answer as to what was helpful. There would be no corporate agreement on what was desirable. But there is a standard by which to judge and it is a standard which we must apply. It is the ultimate criterion, namely the self-disclosure of God who has spoken clearly and decisively to men.

Hebrews 11:6 lays down the basic principles for approaching God: 'Anyone who comes to him must believe that he exists and that he rewards those who earnestly seek him.' At the heart of all true worship is the twofold conviction that God truly exists, and that He is a moral being who honours His promises, carries out His threats and vindicates His Word. All this, however, must be grasped by our minds, and this implies a reverent and an intelligent study of the Scriptures. It means also that while the young convert with the first dawn of spiritual understanding may truly worship God, at the same time a deepening experience of worship will be linked with a deepening understanding. The more we come to know God's character, His purposes and His wishes, the more we will be able to respond to His overtures.

One area where the intellectual aspect is often forgotten is that of praise. It is too readily assumed that the two essential elements of a hymn are the quality of its poetry and the appropriateness of its melody. But while these are important — otherwise we might content ourselves with prose — there is a final standard, namely truth. The ultimate question we ask is whether the hymn reflects and expresses some aspect of biblical truth.

This emphasis is reflected in two of Paul's references to congregational singing. In Colossians 3:16 he roots both teaching and singing in the Word: 'Let the word of Christ dwell in you richly as you teach and admonish one another with all wisdom, and as you sing psalms, hymns and spiritual songs with gratitude in your hearts to God.' This close link of singing with instruction is brought out further in Ephesians

5:19: 'Speak to one another with psalms, hymns and spiritual songs. Sing and make music in your heart to the Lord.' However, if our hymns are to be a vehicle not only of praise to God, but also of instruction, then clearly they must have a doctrinal content which will engage our minds, even as the music stirs our emotions.

The implications are plain. The Scriptures must be central to all we do when we gather as God's people. This centrality of the Word was represented by the older evangelicalism of the Church of England with the insistence that the lectern for the reading of the Bible should be in the very centre of the chancel. One of the by-products of Anglo-Catholicism, which some nonconformists unthinkingly followed, was to push both lectern and pulpit to one side, and to make the communion table central. The older Presbyterian tradition had a custom with a similar emphasis, where the clerk carrying the Bible preceded the minister to the pulpit, indicating that the Scriptures were to govern the proceedings as the worship of the congregation began. We may not wish to emulate these particular observances, but the idea behind them remains valid. The Bible must control us at every point, which is simply another way of saying that the Holy Spirit must control us, for the Scriptures are both His gift to the church, and the instrument by which He controls and blesses the church.

The moral response

As long as a man lives in ignorance of God he will live in ignorance of his sin. This does not mean that he will have no moral scruples, nor that he will not be troubled in conscience. Man made in God's image is a moral being, and no matter how desperately he debases the image, he cannot get away from the basic 'I ought' and 'I ought not' which his Creator has woven into the very fabric of his nature.

Men, however, can go very far down the road of moral decline. Paul gives a grim picture in Romans 1 of a slide into moral corruption and perversion of the most horrible character. He also gives us the reasons for such moral decadence. It comes in the order of the words in verse 18: 'The wrath of God is being revealed from heaven against all the godlessness and wickedness of men who suppress the truth by their wickedness.' In the first place there is ungodliness and then inevitably there follows unrighteousness. Where there is no fear of God there will soon be little respect for men. The final plunge into moral squalor is preceded by spiritual decline. 'Since they did not think it worth while to retain the knowledge of God, he gave them over to a depraved mind, to do what ought not to be done.' Man has suppressed the truth of God and as a result the moral restraints are thrown off.

The reversal of this tragic process begins with the acceptance of the truth which was formerly neglected. As a man is enlightened by the Holy Spirit he begins to understand the Word of God. Now he not only sees God in His holiness and purity, but also himself in his utter sinfulness. Knowledge of the truth and conviction of sin go together, and the first response to the message of the gospel is repentance. This is not, however, a merely backward look of regret for the past. Implicit in true repentance is not only deep sorrow for past sinfulness, but a longing to have done with sin and by God's grace to live a life of holiness.

True worship cannot begin until we have been humbled by the reproof of God. The psalmist frankly acknowledged this truth: 'If I had cherished sin in my heart, the Lord would not have listened' (Ps. 66:18). Earlier, David had made the same point as he faced the question: 'Who may ascend the hill of the Lord? Who may stand in his holy place?' The answer is clear: 'He who has clean hands and a pure heart' (Ps. 24:3,4). The Lord repels both the wilful sinner and the self-righteous hypocrite, but the man who is contrite in spirit is sure of a ready welcome. The Pharisee may stand in the temple courts, but his prayer is in vain and he goes home no different from what he was when he came. The tax collector, by contrast, with his anguished cry, 'God be merciful to me the sinner', is welcomed and forgiven and blessed in soul.

The two aspects of repentance should find their place in the pattern of congregational worship. There is the backward look with its acknowledgement of sinful failure, not only in terms of doing what we ought not to have done, but also of leaving undone what we ought to have done. But repentance, while it frankly confesses sins of commission and omission, also has a forward look. Beyond the renewed experience of pardon and cleansing there is the next step of obedience. Penitence is the prelude to renewed consecration with its accompanying desire to know and do the will of God.

The note of penitence is struck as the congregation is led in confession of sin. It is present in the constant refrain, as the Scriptures are read, and the holy God calls His people to holy living. It is demanded by the Spirit of God as the sermon is preached. It is expressed for many a penitent in a reading of one of the penitential psalms or in the singing of such a hymn as that of John Newton:

> Bowed down beneath a load of sin;
> By Satan sorely pressed,
> By war without and fears within,
> I come to thee for rest.

Penitence points forward to obedience. The chastening experience of being rebuked by the Spirit of God leads us to rejoice afresh in the cleansing of the blood of Christ. It leads us also to fresh spiritual resolve. Again it is often in the singing of one of the great hymns of the church that this aspiration for holiness and desire for faithful service find their deepest expression. How often believers have emerged from a self-humbling encounter with God with Philip Doddridge's words on their lips:

> My gracious Lord, I own Thy right
> To every service I can pay
> And call it my supreme delight
> To hear Thy dictates and obey.

The emotional response

God made us, not only creatures who think and act, but also those who feel. We smile and we frown; we are moved to laughter and to tears; there is an inner warmth and also a chill in our spirits; we can be exuberant and we can be dejected; we may be stirred at a concert to enthusiastic applause or we may share a general feeling of disappointment and torpor. In short our emotions play a major part in our lives.

The two basic emotions are those associated with pleasure and pain. When something pleases us our feelings impel us to continue in the situation, or to move in the direction where the source of pleasure is to be found. When we encounter pain, whether physical or mental, our feelings are hurt and there is an instinctive reaction, so that we want to get away as far as possible from the source of our distress. In a sense, pleasure and pain are two aspects of the instinct of self-preservation. We cultivate any experience or circumstance which leads to our well-being, and avoid any pattern of events likely to cause us harm. Put in very basic terms, men are constituted in such a way that they desire happiness, and try to avoid unhappiness.

While the Spirit of God speaks in the first place to the mind, we must never construe that as meaning that He does not also utilize our feelings as He leads us from our self-centred sinfulness to faith in Christ. He confronts us with the truths of God and He uses them to probe our conscience and so to move us to repentance. But, because we are complete persons, He is working at the same time in the area of our feelings. For the purpose of clear thinking we may distinguish between the different aspects of the Spirit's activity, but in reality our nature does not consist of a number of watertight compartments. While the Spirit may more obviously be exerting pressure on one part of us, His presence is at the same time being felt throughout.

We can see this if we examine some of our fundamental spiritual experiences. Repentance is not some detached and rather dispassionate analysis of our moral weakness, with an accompanying assessment of our sin and guilt. It is inevitably accompanied by sorrow, and may indeed end in bitter tears. This is due to the fact that we are not examining ourselves in terms of an impersonal code of laws which unhappily we have violated. Rather we have grievously sinned against a Person, the gracious Creator who gave us life and breath and all we have, and whom we have requited with ugly ingratitude. So, as the Spirit convicts us of sin, He not only displays to our conscience the breaches of God's law for which we are guilty, he makes us feel the wretchedness of our own rebellion against a loving God.

Faith also has its emotional content. It is true that it is essentially a response to the Word of God. We hear that Word preached, and we respond by accepting it and acting upon it. But such acceptance is no mere nod of mental assent to a series of religious propositions. The focal point of all Scripture is the Lord Jesus Christ. To respond in faith to the word of the gospel is to turn in trust to Christ. But because such trust is personal reliance on Him who suffered and died for sinners, it cannot be divorced from warm gratitude and deep shame that it was our sin which caused His pain. To say that faith means trust is to say that, with all its intellectual content and its moral reaction, it also has an emotional dimension. We believe in Him with all our heart!

A deepening knowledge of the God whom we have come to know in Christ will not only enlarge our mental horizon, it will also stir us deeply. The more we scale the heights of truth, the more we shall be like the climber in the Alps who is overwhelmed by the glory of the panorama of snowy peaks cutting into the blueness of the sky. So we search the Scriptures and discover what a vast terrain of truth we have yet to traverse. At the same time each new discovery brings with it fresh delights, because it ushers us into the presence of a friend whom we are learning to know with an increasing intimacy.

To bow in prayer and praise, or to join with the congregation in adoration and thanksgiving, is to know a deep stirring of our emotions. It is not only that the truth grips us and moves us. There is also the fact of fellowship with other Christians who are united with us in a common desire to know and to worship God. We were not made for a solitary existence but for the common life of a shared human experience. Sin has entered as a disruptive and divisive element, setting man against man, and producing bitterness, strife and discord. It is one of the marks of the new life in Christ that we discover our links with a fellowship of people who are joined to us by a bond which is much stronger than that of a mere shared interest. We belong together, and in that shared experience we stimulate one another. It is not surprising, therefore, that as we join in worship our emotional response is intensified and deepened by the obvious moving of the Spirit of God in the gathered company of believers.

It is important to notice a vital distinction between a healthy stirring of the emotions and emotionalism. The latter is present when a technique is employed which sidesteps the mind and ignores the moral implications of the gospel. It is sadly evident in some meetings, where the atmosphere is deliberately created by means of music or conditioning humour, to make people susceptible. It may also be employed by the preacher who uses a moving story not simply as an illustration but as a means of emotional manipulation. It is all too often the instrument which levers people out of their seats to respond to an appeal which has been accompanied by the soft singing of a choir, and reinforced by the powerful suggestion of the apparent response of others.

All such emotionalism is wrong for it ignores the totality of man's nature. It elicits a response, but it is only a partial one. It can lead to a tragic reaction of disillusionment and bitterness when, after the passing of the religious excitement, normal life resumes with its difficulties, its drab monotony or its personal problems. Even when, in spite of the misuse of such methods, a person truly comes to faith in Christ, there may be a sad legacy in that someone whose conversion was accomplished in such an emotionally overcharged way may remain partially dependent on such stimuli. The premature spiritual birth may lead to a condition of arrested development in which some new emotional fillip is constantly required. Even more seriously, emotionalism may lead a person to a spurious profession and anaesthetize him so that he is satisfied with his condition, and becomes immune to the real demands of the gospel.

A healthy stirring of the emotions is produced by the truth of God applied by the Holy Spirit to the mind and conscience and will. It is from that impact of the Word that the deepest emotional experiences emerge, and it is here that we find the secret of the depth of feeling associated in Scripture with true worship. It was this appreciation of the truth which led the psalmist to tears of repentance. It was truth also which stirred him to joy and gladness, and at times to exaltation of spirit. A false emotionalism acts like a drug which dulls the sensitivities even while it seems to stimulate, so that the addict needs more frequent and stronger doses. A true emotional stirring is one that not only stimulates us to worship, but deepens our spiritual zest and gives us a capacity as well as a passionate desire for deeper experiences of the fulness of God.

It is possible to err in this matter in different ways. There are congregations where the stress is all on objective truth. There is little scope for emotional release and the result is a people who are strong in doctrinal knowledge, but apparently

dull in spirit. The service of worship in such a situation can
become frigid and lifeless. At the other extreme are those
who live in a state of constantly induced excitement. The
subjective element has taken over as the objective has receded.
The result is a sorry condition of superficiality where all too
often people are ready to grasp at any new novelty, and to be
led astray by all kinds of doctrinal aberrations.

The condition which leads to a healthy emotional reaction
is one where there is a balance between the objective and the
subjective. The great truths of Scripture are firmly enunciated,
and preached with authority; and the pattern of worship is
tested by scriptural principles. At the same time there is a
recognition that people have emotional needs, so there is provision for the expression of deep feeling, and a vigorous
attempt to reject the formal practices of some rigid tradition
which would inhibit true spontaneity in worship.

This blend of the objective and the subjective, of the doctrinal statement and the inner response, is seen in the great
hymns of the church. They are not only theologically correct
but they move us in the depths of our souls. They give us a
clear understanding of some aspect of God's revelation and at
the same time fire our hearts and put on our lips an adequate
expression of the delight which has flooded us. Not for them
the shallowness of many modern or late Victorian religious
ditties which are obsessed with the singer's own personal
moods expressed in terms of sugared sentiment. Their theme
is rather the grandeur and majesty of the truth of God, eliciting from the adoring worshipper the response of awe and
reverence, of grateful love and exultant praise. By way of
illustration, and by way also of a fitting close to this consideration of the emotional aspect of worship we could
scarcely do better than quote the opening and closing verses
of Thomas Oliver's magnificent hymn of praise:

> The God of Abraham praise,
> Who reigns enthroned above,
> Ancient of everlasting days,
> And God of love.
> Jehovah! Great I AM!
> By earth and heaven confessed,
> I bow and bless the sacred name
> For ever blessed.

The whole triumphant host
Give thanks to God on high,
'Hail, Father, Son and Holy Ghost!'
They ever cry.
Hail, Abraham's God, and mine!
I join the heavenly lays.
All might and majesty are Thine,
And endless praise.

The aesthetic response

To appreciate beauty is to be a normal human being! Man not only thinks and feels and wills; he also responds to what is beautiful. There are indeed differences between individuals, and between various national groups, as to what constitutes beauty, but at the same time there is a basic agreement. The precise reaction to different aromas or sounds or sights will vary with each person's sensitivities, ability and education. But then the same is true of intellectual reactions, in that one may find pleasure in reading the potted contents of a popular newspaper, while another may find his enjoyment in cryptic crosswords or chess problems. However, both the unlearned and the highly educated share a common human ability to think. So, too, men in general react to what they consider beautiful, even though they might disagree deeply about its precise definition. To meet a person who thought that the smell of an open sewer was lovely, or who considered the rusty tins and plastic bags of a city dump a pleasing spectacle, or who equated with good music the sound of a broken-down piano being battered by a child — this would not lead to the conclusion that there is no such thing as beauty, but rather that the person concerned was mentally sick.

It is true that, in a sense, 'Beauty is in the eye of the beholder', but that needs to be qualified. A sunset on a desert island has the same light and shade as the one on a neighbouring island where there is a colony of artists. A skylark sings the same song when there is no human ear to listen. There is also the further qualification, that appreciation of beauty may be developed. A student can learn about art or music, and so come to a deeper appreciation of it. Yet, when we have made all our qualifications, it still remains true that there is in our human nature a built-in response to beauty.

This is not surprising, since man was made in the image of God, for God clearly loves beauty. It was He after all who with a liberal hand decked the world which He created with the staggering variety of flowers and shrubs, of brilliant plumage and magnificent animal furs, of mountain and lake, of dawn's pink and sunset's crimson. It was He who taught a nightingale to sing and He who gave men and women the gift of speech and song. Such indeed is God's love of beauty that he has poured out His artistic work in the loveliness of nature even when, as in the case of submarine life or of microscopic beauties long hidden, there was no appreciative human audience to see.

Man in the image of God both appreciates and also creates beauty. Just as he knows the difference between intelligent speech and nonsense, or recognizes the difference between right and wrong, so he can see the gulf between what is beautiful and what is ugly. Beauty means harmony. It is a condition where there are no discordant or harsh or jarring features. The simplest tune has some element of beauty whereas a cacophony of discordant notes is only an unpleasant din. Then also beauty means symmetry in which there is an appropriateness between the different elements in a picture or a structure or a piece of music. Lack of balance or lack of coherence can be ugly whereas an orderly blend of colours or of sounds is beautiful. A woman wearing colours which clash violently is not a pleasing spectacle; but the harmonious blend of all the varieties of colour in a herbaceous border is lovely. A shrill and flat soprano singing loudly and stridently above a choir can be excruciating to the hearer, whereas the balance of all the parts will bring great delight.

As in every other area of human life, sin has brought its blighting effects. Man the thinker is darkened in his understanding by sin. Man the worker is perverted by his sinful selfishness. So too, man, the reflector of the Creator who loves beauty, has been affected in his aesthetic sense. Thus his self-centred condition is shown even in his enjoyment of beautiful music or art, in that he gives no thought to the God who is the ultimate source of the skill of the musician or the artist. Then again he reflects his own spiritual state in the art which he produces. Influenced by faith in the living God he can create works of art which move us deeply. But estranged from God, and in the mood of despair so frequent today, he may produce discordant music and grotesque paintings as a reflex of his own feeling of the absurdity of existence. Above all, he shows his sinfulness when he makes beauty an end in itself. Idolatry, as Paul showed in Romans 1, is the outcome of man's sin, in that he worships the creation rather than the Creator. So men talk of 'art for art's sake' as if art or any other activity could ever be an end in itself, rather than one more vehicle to express the glory of God.

One outcome of the revolutionary change which the gospel calls spiritual rebirth, is a new appreciation of beauty. A man may have enjoyed music or art or landscapes before; indeed he may have been an instructed art critic before. Now, however, he can see and hear so much more. He is seeing the evidence of the God of beauty at work in the world. The colours, the light and shade, the musical sounds — all now stir his soul to a deeper appreciation than he ever knew before, and so he bows in worship.

Nor is it only in the natural world, or in the beauties of artistic creations, that he finds a new delight. He begins to appreciate also the beauty and glory of God Himself. The harmony of God's attributes, where holiness and mercy and power and wisdom all blend into a glorious unity, fill him with delight. The marvellous coherence of the elements of the gospel and of the great work of redemption stir him as a man is moved by the intricate beauties of a great architectural achievement.

Now also he detects a beauty in Christ and His work which he did not see before. Formerly his attitude could be summed up in Isaiah's acknowledgement of the common reaction to the suffering Servant: 'He had no beauty or majesty to attract us to him, nothing in his appearance that we should desire him' (Isa. 53:2). Now, however, he sees a beauty which transfigures the suffering Servant. It is not the kind of beauty in suffering conceived by artists, who have tried to represent a Jesus about whose physical features and appearance the Holy Spirit has maintained a steady silence. Rather it is the beauty of His character and the glory of His work which grip the soul. So the believer comes to realize why Christians have found the passionate love lyrics of the Song of Solomon a fitting expression of their appreciative delight in the great

Lover of their souls. Matson's hymn well expresses the change of attitude:

> Lord I was blind: I could not see
> In Thy marred visage any grace,
> But now the beauty of Thy face
> In radiant vision dawns on me.

When Jesus claimed, 'I am the good shepherd,' the Greek word used in John 10:11 is *kalos,* which has, as a basic element in its meaning, the idea of beauty. Plato, the Greek philosopher, in writing of his ideal world, pictured the supreme Idea as *'To Kalon'* and in this he viewed the combination of the three elements – the good, the true and the beautiful. The supreme ideal thus combined moral splendour and beauty. It is with this background that we can see the richness of the word which describes the Lord Jesus. He is not only morally good and faithfully consistent, but there is a beauty in Him which elicits a response of praise, and moves us to pray for a deeper appreciation of His loveliness. Samuel Rutherford, the seventeenth-century Scottish Covenanter, has a typically picturesque statement of this truth: 'There are curtains in the loveliness of Christ not yet drawn aside.' To worship the Lord 'in the beauty of holiness', or, as it may be rendered, 'in the splendour of his holiness' is to respond with delight as the Holy Spirit draws aside the curtains to reveal the glory yet unseen.

This implies that our appreciation of the beauty of the Lord, both in the work of creation and of redemption, is to be developed. Like any art or music student, we are to grow, not only in our understanding, but in our corresponding response. Paul stresses the point in his letter to the Philippians as he urges us to use our minds to cultivate our knowledge of all the aspects of God's truth. It is in that context that he urges us to develop our aesthetic appreciation of God: 'Whatever is lovely – think about such things' (Phil. 4:8). Such a cultivation is achieved as we open our minds to the Scriptures under the direction of the Spirit, and as we meet in the stimulating fellowship of those who are engaged in the same quest to see more of the beauties of the Lord.

Those with whom we meet for worship on the Lord's Day represent the usual cross-section of any social group. There are the young and the old, the rich and the poor, the clever and the ordinary, the healthy and the sick. Here is a variety of temperament and outlook, and here also a bewildering variety of strengths and weaknesses, of attractive features and unattractive failings. Yet here in this ordinary group of finite and evidently sinful mortals, the glory of God may be seen. Here we see in one man the evidence of the moral change which the grace of God can effect. There is another who in men's judgement would be counted ugly, yet the face is transfigured by an inner beauty of soul. Here is an old person whose wrinkled face only serves to highlight the joyful twinkle of the eyes. There is a group of young people whose eager zeal is more than a mere youthful enthusiasm. It is in the beauty of such a worshipping congregation that we see a pale reflection of the glory of their Saviour, and in their song of praise we hear a faint echo of the tones of the great Head of the church.

Self-deception is, however, always a sad possibility in our times of worship. We may delude ourselves that we are responding to the preaching of the Word, when in fact we are simply enjoying the intellectual stimulus of a cogently argued presentation of Christian doctrine. We may imagine that we are being stirred to fresh resolve and new endeavour, when we are only emotionally moved by a congregation apparently united in a hymn of submission. So, too, we may confuse a mere aesthetic reaction with a truly worshipping response. After all, a scoffing atheist may be deeply stirred by the glory of a sunset, and the most godless man may be lost in wonder in face of the magnificence of King's College Chapel. But in either case they are simply indicating that being human they respond to beauty; they are not worshipping the God who dressed that landscape or who gave the stonemasons the skill to mould that exquisite fan vaulting in the chapel roof. To move beyond mere appreciation to true worship involves not only opening our eyes to see the beauty before us, but opening the eye of faith to see the greater beauty beyond.

This means that much care must be exercised to avoid distracting the worshipper from his supreme task. There is much talk about the use of the visual arts in worship, whereas in fact they can be a major hindrance to us. There is a significant change in this area from the Old Testament pattern to the

New. In the Old Testament there was much emphasis on the external forms and on the furnishing of the place of worship. There were the colours of the dyed skins on the tabernacle and later the sumptuous beauty of the temple. There was the gold of the table and the vessels, the bronze of the altar, the magnificence of the priestly vestments, the lights and the incense. Sadly, for many the external beauties proved to be, not a pathway to God, but an ornate cul-de-sac. Increasingly the prophets warn against an empty and formal worship and call for a response which reaches beyond the seen to the unseen.

With the advent of the gospel there is no longer any fixed place for worship. It is, said Jesus to the woman of Samaria, 'neither on this mountain nor in Jerusalem' that God is to be worshipped. There is no need for outward splendour, for a specially garbed minister, or for such symbolic additions as candles or incense. Now the emphasis is on order and simplicity, and these can be achieved in whatever situation Christians meet. It may be in a mediaeval church or a well-constructed modern chapel; it may be in someone's lounge or in the local community centre; but wherever it is, the congregation may sing:

> Jesus, where'er Thy people meet,
> There they behold Thy mercy seat;
> Where'er they seek Thee, Thou art found,
> And every place is hallowed ground.

Obviously it would be absurd to go to the other extreme and to cultivate ugliness for its own sake, for it can be as big a distraction as beauty. We can be deflected from true worship not only by attractive features in a building but also by those which irritate. We are still human and our normal faculties remain in operation. A painfully uncomfortable chair will hinder our concentration, and a dingy and poorly lit hall will be no great asset! It is natural for us to appreciate a comfortable and aesthetically pleasing building. We must, however, remember that this is not an essential requisite for worship but simply a natural provision for human needs. If we believe that the preaching of the Word and the concentration of the minds of the worshippers are of prime concern, then such factors as acoustics and ventilation are of greater importance than architectural elegance! The peril of idolatry is an ever-present one, as the Old Testament so clearly reveals. We must therefore guard against anything being introduced, which lowers our gaze from the glory of our God to the lesser glories of our own artistic creations.

The worship of the church in this realm, as in all others, is an anticipation of the praise of heaven. There the rich symbolism of the Apocalypse discloses the beauties which already stir the heavenly choir, and which await those of us who have not yet joined the church triumphant. There is the full-throated song of a vast congregation with perfect harmony and with no discordant note. There is the city of unimaginable beauty with its gates of pearl and its streets of gold. There is the radiance of an eternal light which eclipses the glory of the most wonderful earthly dawn or sunset. Above all, at the heart of everything, stands the throne of God set on a sea of glass, with an emerald rainbow of mercy around the throne. There enthroned is the Lord of the universe and there also is the Lamb in all His glory.

This is the final beauty. It is a vision of such richness and depth and fulness, that day and night unceasingly the choir of the redeemed continues in praise, seeing so much and finding more to see, exulting and yet finding still more to charm their hearts. Samuel Rutherford in his lonely exile in St Andrews, far from his beloved people, could comfort himself with the prospect of an even more glorious worship than they had enjoyed together in Anwoth, as he contemplated the glory of Immanuel's land. Anne Ross Cousin caught his mood and well reflected it in her hymn which reaches its climax in the closing verse:

> The King there in His beauty,
> Without a veil is seen;
> It were a well-spent journey,
> Though seven deaths lay between:
> The Lamb with His fair army,
> Doth on Mount Zion stand,
> And glory, glory dwelleth
> In Immanuel's land.

The physical response

Since there are scarcely any human activities which do not involve some physical accompaniment, it is obvious that engaging in worship involves our bodies. When we sing praise we use our lips and our lungs. When we pray we stand or sit or kneel. When we participate in the Lord's supper we engage in the very physical activity of eating and drinking. Then also we are affected by our bodily states. If we are tired or unwell, if the building is overheated or badly ventilated, if the acoustics are poor or the pews uncomfortable, we will find these factors a distraction. We are, after all, not disembodied spirits but men and women of flesh and blood.

It is true that in many of our everyday activities we are not consciously aware of the physical actions we employ. When we turn the pages of a newspaper or switch on the light or lift a cup of tea, we do so almost automatically. There are, however, occasions when the physical act is quite deliberate. We may pick up an umbrella on a wet day without giving any thought to the muscular functioning of our hands, but the Olympic athlete will pick up his javelin with careful deliberation before he throws it. We may chat to a friend without bothering about our articulation, but the professional singer will pay careful attention to breathing and posture. There are, in short, actions which are virtually involuntary and there are others which are deliberate. Furthermore, there are actions which convey meaning. We may stamp our feet on a cold day simply to restore our circulation, but an audience may stamp their feet in appreciation of a performance.

When we meet together for worship there are physical actions which are in the category of the incidental, and others which are deliberate and meaningful. But we are not always aware of the difference, for what we may consider to be a normal posture or action, which we do as a matter of routine, may be to another worshipping group quite unusual. We may assume, for example, that it is the obvious thing to do when we stand to sing, until we visit a church where they sit to sing. We may think that to sit at the Lord's table is the natural thing to do until we discuss the issue with Anglican friends who kneel. It is simply a fact that different Christians and different congregations adopt specific physical actions to accompany their worship, and in their uses they vary considerably.

It should not come as a surprise that bodily factors enter into our worship. For one thing, our Creator has made us as we are, not only with minds and emotions, but also with lips and eyes, with hands and feet. To use our limbs to glorify Him is simply to function as the Creator designed us. Then also the body of the Christian has become in Paul's words, 'the temple of the Holy Spirit'. The phrase recalls the Old Testament where the very structure of the temple was designed to glorify God. So the limbs of the Christian's body, the constituent elements of the spiritual temple, are instruments to be employed for the glory of God. This will affect our attitude to work and leisure and indeed to all our activities. Whatever we do, we must aim to glorify God. It will also influence us as we consider more specifically personal and corporate worship. Here we will view our bodily powers as a means to enrich the worship of our hearts. We worship in spirit and in truth; but as those who are still in this earthly condition of flesh and blood we also use all our powers of mind and of body to magnify our God. Martin Rinkart's hymn gives the pattern:

> Now thank we all our God
> With hearts and hands and voices.

What posture then shall we adopt for prayer — shall we stand or sit or kneel? The answer of Scripture is not an endorsement of any particular posture for it gives examples of all three being employed. Admittedly the evidence for the practice of remaining seated is very scanty. It is true that Moses sat to pray on Mount Horeb, but it was only because he had become tired standing (Exod. 17:12). However, when David prayed (2 Sam. 7:18) he 'sat before the Lord', and there is no suggestion that this was due to any other factor than as a prelude to prayer. Standing for prayer is, however, much more frequent, especially in the Old Testament. 'Abraham remained standing before the Lord' (Gen. 18:22) as he pleaded for those in Sodom. Hannah recalls to Eli her prayer in the house of the Lord: 'I am the woman who stood here beside you praying to the Lord' (1 Sam. 1:26). The psalmist speaks of standing in the courts of the Lord (Ps. 24:3; 134:1; 135:2).

Jesus envisaged men praying thus when He gave His disciples instructions about prayer — 'When you stand praying' (Mark 11:25) — and when He described the Pharisee and the tax collector at prayer in the temple (Luke 18:11,13).

Of kneeling for prayer there is much evidence, and it is particularly noticeable that this practice is much more marked in the New Testament. This is not to say that there are no examples in the Old Testament, for Solomon knelt to pray at the dedication of the temple (1 Kings 8:54). Daniel obviously knelt as his normal pattern (Dan. 6:10); and the psalmist summons us to worship: 'Come let us bow down in worship, let us kneel before the Lord our Maker' (Ps. 95:6). However, in the New Testament it is this posture which is especially prominent.

Luke recalls that Jesus knelt in Gethsemane (Luke 22:41) and it may be that this sacred association of kneeling at prayer led Luke to mention the fact specifically on different occasions in the Acts. So he recalls that Stephen 'fell on his knees' to pray for his murderers (Acts 7:60); that Peter knelt to pray for the restoration of Dorcas (9:40); that Paul and the Ephesian elders knelt together for prayer (20:36); and — perhaps the most striking example, in view of the location — he describes the scene at Tyre when the crowd of disciples with wives and children came to say farewell to Paul, and all of them knelt down on the beach (21:5).

Not surprisingly, when Paul wrote the letter to the Ephesians he prefaced his prayer for them with the statement: 'I kneel before the Father' (Eph. 3:14). The vision of the final glory of Christ has a similar emphasis as he looks forward to that day when 'every knee shall bow . . . and every tongue confess that Jesus Christ is Lord' (Phil. 2:10-11).

We may draw certain conclusions from these various biblical references. In the first place no one posture may be prescribed as the only correct one. To think along these lines is to move towards a legalism which becomes so taken up with the outward action that it obscures, or even forgets, the essential spiritual response. There are times when standing is the only normal posture — the commuter in a London tube is not called on to kneel in order to turn his heart to God, nor if a worshipper remains seated in a chapel, where crowded conditions make kneeling a physical impossibility, should he feel that he is lacking in reverence or fervour. At the same time we do need to notice how much our attention is drawn in Scripture to the practice of kneeling for prayer, and we may need to adapt our own practice accordingly, always with the reflection that if the spirit is not bowed before God no amount of physical kneeling will be a substitute for true humility.

What we do with our hands when we pray also receives quite a degree of attention in the Bible. The gesture to which our notice is specially drawn is that of stretching out our hands or of raising them in supplication or in praise. Moses lifted his hands to God in prayer and recalled the significance of the gesture by building an altar, and making the comment: 'Hands were lifted up to the throne of the Lord' (Exod. 17:16). Solomon, to whose prayer of dedication reference has already been made, not only knelt but spread out his hands towards heaven (1 Kings 8:54). When Ezra summoned the people to praise God they 'lifted their hands and responded "Amen! Amen!"' (Neh. 8:6.)

Raising the hands is also a characteristic feature of prayer and praise in the Psalms. So, David cries for mercy: 'I lift up my hands towards your Most Holy Place' (Ps. 28:2). He praises God for all His goodness: 'I will praise you as long as I live, and in your name I will lift up my hands' (Ps. 63:4). The call to those who minister in the house of the Lord is in the same vein: 'Lift up your hands in the sanctuary and praise the Lord' (Ps. 134:2). Prayer is pictured as incense rising to God and the lifting up of the hands 'like the evening sacrifice' (141:2). Jeremiah, in the agony of his lamentation over Jerusalem, speaks vividly of lifting the hands in prayer: 'Pour out your heart like water in the presence of the Lord. Lift up your hands to him for the lives of your children . . . Let us lift up our hearts and our hands to God in heaven' (Lam. 2:19; 3:41).

With this wealth of biblical references one can more fully appreciate Paul's word to Timothy: 'I want men everywhere to lift up holy hands in prayer, without anger or disputing' (1 Tim. 2:8). The physical gesture suggests an awareness of the transcendence of God. He is above and beyond us and so we stretch out our hands and lift up our hearts to Him. Yet it is no despairing act, for though our hands are empty, in acknowledgement of our utter dependence on Him, they are raised in complete trust, and also in glad appreciation of the source of all our good. It suggests also the hands of the lover stretched out to embrace the object of his passionate desire. It reminds us also of the sobering requirements of the God whom we worship. To come to Him demands 'clean hands and a pure heart' (Ps. 24:4). The hands which Paul wishes to see raised in prayer must be 'holy hands'. Our hands are the instruments we use in our daily work, in our leisure and in our general activities. If we are to raise holy hands in prayer and praise, we need constantly to humble ourselves before God, so that with a fresh experience of His pardoning love and cleansing mercy we may come to Him with confidence.

Clapping, which is much favoured in some circles, has very little scriptural support. There are some references to clapping in the Bible, all of them in the Old Testament. Five of them refer to hand-clapping as a mark of derision; two of them are metaphorical, picturing the rivers and the trees rejoicing before God; one is a reference to the applause which greeted the accession of Joash as king. In only one case is there a specific reference to people worshipping with such an accompaniment: 'Clap your hands, all you nations; shout to God with cries of joy' (Ps. 47:1). It was the kind of response which was seen at the coronation of a king and so it fits into the context of the jubilation of spirit which responds to the glory of Jehovah's sovereign power. This one reference to this kind of applause may be a sufficient justification for those who wish to express their exuberance in this way. At the same time the silence of most of the Bible, and especially of the New Testament, suggests that what is not justified is an undue emphasis on the practice. We must accord freedom to those who wish to clap their hands in joyful worship; but let us resist any tendency to impose hand-clapping as a kind of liturgical routine.

Turning our attention from hands to feet, we encounter the debate as to the role of the dance in worship. Some would argue that rhythmic bodily movements are a very natural human reaction — witness the spontaneous dancing of small children and the widespread, if not universal, practice of the art across the world. Allied to this argument from human needs and responses is an appeal to the biblical evidence as a justification for the introduction — or as its advocates would claim, a reintroduction — of dancing into public worship.

Certainly there is evidence in the Old Testament that joyful dancing was used to express praise and thanksgiving. When Pharaoh's host was overwhelmed in the Red Sea, Miriam, who is described as 'a prophetess' not only led the people in victorious song but took a tambourine and led the women in their music and dancing (Exod. 15:20). The scene was recalled centuries later when Jeremiah prophesied the return of Israel from exile: 'Again you will take up your tambourines and go out to dance with the joyful' (Jer. 31:4). When David brought the ark of the Lord to Jerusalem he was obviously stirred to the depths, and to the intense disapproval of his wife, cast off his inhibitions, and 'danced before the Lord with all his might' (2 Sam. 6:16; 1 Chron. 15:29).

Perhaps even more significant are the references in the Psalms, for they refer to dancing as an established element in worship. The dancing of Miriam or of David may be explained as exuberant outbursts on very special occasions. But in Psalms 149:3 and 150:4 the context is a call to worship, and the references are not to something unusual, but to a practice which was both known and normally practised in the temple. H. C. Leupold in his *Exposition of the Psalms* prefers to translate the word in Psalm 150:4 as 'solemn dance' in order 'to recall the distinctive nature of this type of liturgical action'. W. S. Plumer in his commentary on the Psalms wrote that, 'The dance was in early times one of the modes of expressing religious joy.' The bearing of this on his own situation Plumer did not consider, on the grounds that in his time dancing was not used for religious purposes and until that happened there was no need to discuss the subject! However, as far as we are concerned, the situation which Plumer did not face now exists, namely the widespread renewal of dancing in worship. So we must do what he felt he did not need to do — consider the practice seriously.

In view of the strong evidence of the Old Testament that dancing was a familiar expression of worship, the silence of the New Testament is all the more striking. Of dancing as an act of worship there is no example, nor is there any command or even a word of sanction for the practice. There are two examples of dancing in the Gospels, one of them being the children's games which the Lord used as an illustration (Matt. 11:17; Luke 7:32) and the other the dancing of Herodias' daughter (Matt. 14:6; Mark 6:22) which was a far cry from anything religious! There are two references in the Acts to men dancing for joy after experiencing the power of God; but then both of them had been healed after being crippled from birth (Acts 3:8; 14:10). It was hardly surprising that men finding power in their legs for the first time in their life should leap with delight, nor was it surprising that the Spirit should have moved them in this way as it was a public demonstration of the reality of their physical healing.

When, however, we turn to the descriptions of the church at worship, whether in the Acts or the Epistles, and when we examine the apostolic teaching we find no hint of a liturgical dance. This is not perhaps so surprising when we recall the context of the early Christians, living as they did with the twin influences of Greek and Roman culture. Both with the Greeks and the Romans, dancing was primarily a religious ceremonial, and Plato thought that all dancing should have this religious character. Dancing as a spectacle was known, with dancing-girls providing the entertainment, but the Romans had little time for it unless it was a religious exercise. Indeed that is one of the reasons why the Emperor Nero, with his love of dancing, was so despised. Since the dance was thus, both in Greek and Roman society, identified with pagan worship, and so inevitably with immorality, it is no wonder that it finds no place in the New Testament.

If someone has just experienced a miraculous healing like the cripple at the temple gate or the lame man at Lystra, we would not be surprised to see him leap for joy. Indeed it would be understandable if someone came powerfully under the influence of the Holy Spirit and behaved like Christian in *Pilgrim's Progress* who, having lost his burden at the cross, 'gave three leaps for joy'. It is, however, one thing to allow freedom for a Christian to show his joy in a spontaneous way; it is quite another to produce the kind of choreography which is today the preparation for what is termed 'spiritual dancing'. To quote the spiritual illiteracy of twentieth-century man and the value of a dramatic presentation of the gospel is to face the counter-arguments that first-century man according to Paul was equally ignorant (1 Cor. 2:14); that the dance, so

readily available in Greek and Roman society, was never sug-
gested; and that, far from clarifying the gospel, the dance has
itself to be explained by means of the very words which it is
supposed to be making plain!

We return to our starting-point. Worship is essentially a
spiritual exercise in which the spirit of man meets the living
God and bows in praise and prayer. Because we are still in
the body, physical accompaniments are inevitable. They
must, however, always be seen as entirely auxiliary to the
spiritual activity. To let them gain undue prominence, or to
concentrate attention on what you do with hands or feet, is
to move in the direction of a barren and formal externalism.
While it may help us to kneel for prayer, the mere act of
kneeling is no substitution for a humble and contrite spirit.
While the worshipper may raise the hands in prayer, the
physical act will be an empty gesture if it is not accompanied
by purity of heart. Because God has given us our bodies to
use for His glory, and because his Spirit makes these bodies
His temple, we will want to employ all our powers to extol
our God. The apostle reminds us of the right emphasis and
also the correct order in our worship: 'Offer yourselves to
God, as those who have been brought from death to life;
and offer the parts of your body to him as instruments of
righteousness' (Rom. 6:13).

5 The place of the sermon

There has been a tendency in some circles to draw a distinction between worship and preaching. At one extreme there is a celebration of the Lord's supper without the ministry of the Word, as if the latter were an optional extra. At the other end of the ecclesiastical spectrum reference is made to what precedes the preaching as 'the preliminaries', as if the prayer and praise of the congregation were secondary considerations. However, to separate the preaching from the general pattern of worship is not to elevate the sermon but to fail to see the total picture.

Worship, as we have seen, is in spirit and in truth. It is directed to the true God and is offered in the way declared by Him. This means that the stimulus to worship is the presentation of the truth; and the control of the pattern of worship is also the preaching of the Word. Without preaching, worship can degenerate into a mere liturgical routine, or can be a well-orchestrated method of emotional release by a leader well versed in methods of conditioning people. Thus to introduce the subject of preaching is not to digress from the main theme of this book. It is rather to discuss an issue which is fundamental if our worship is to be informed, balanced and alive.

Nor is a consideration of preaching a matter of interest only to preachers. To view a congregation as being merely passive recipients of a spoken word, is to put a sermon in the same category as a lecture or an after-dinner speech. But it is totally different, not simply in the nature and content of the sermon, but in the interaction of preacher and hearers. The congregation plays a vital role in the preaching, as any preacher will freely acknowledge, knowing as he does the vast difference between a responsive people replying from their hearts to the Word, and a passive congregation who are fulfilling their normal Sunday routine. Indeed, it is true to say that good congregations make for good preaching, for they stimulate the preacher to prepare adequately and lift him to heights in the pulpit beyond his normal powers. It is, of course, the activity of the Holy Spirit which explains this, for He who makes the congregation His temple also fires the heart and unlooses the tongue of the preacher.

Because the congregation plays an active role it is important that they should know the character of preaching, and so appreciate what they should expect when, to use the classic Puritan phrase, 'they sit under the Word'. Jesus Himself gave two allied commands on this issue: 'Consider carefully what you hear' (Mark 4:24) and 'Consider carefully how you listen' (Luke 8:18). So the hearer is to pay heed, both to the content and to the way in which it is presented, and so to the way in which he should respond. He is not called to an acquiescence in which all that the preacher says is accepted uncritically. It is true that the preacher has the authority of one commissioned by the Holy Spirit. But his commission does not confer infallibility, nor does it deliver him from the after-effects of overwork nor, sadly, from his own lapses into slackness in preparation. The hearer must therefore emulate the people of Berea who are so warmly commended by Luke because they tested what Paul preached by reference to the Scriptures.

The preacher

How then should the preacher approach his task, and how should the congregation view their responsibility as they pray for him, and as they prepare themselves to hear the Word of God? In the first place preaching must be seen as a divinely appointed means of blessing, and so of eliciting from those who hear the response of repentance, faith and obedience. The preacher in the New Testament is a herald whose task is similar to that of the servant of an oriental king, whose arrival in one of his towns was announced by the herald's trumpet. So the preacher sounds the trumpet-blast of the gospel to arouse sinners from their slumber, and to call God's people to holiness of life. Paul uses the word which describes the herald's task when he writes to the Corinthians, 'We preach Christ crucified.' He acknowledges that preaching is to the outsider an exercise of folly, but he insists that it is God's way of working: 'God was pleased through the foolishness of what was preached to save those who believe' (1 Cor. 1:21). His preaching was no mere exercise of human ability or eloquence, but was delivered 'with a demonstration of the Spirit's power' (1 Cor. 2:4). He echoes this note in writing to the Thessalonians where he claims that his preaching came 'not simply with words, but also with power, with the Holy Spirit and with deep conviction' (1 Thess. 1:5). The final charge to his young disciple Timothy reinforces the emphasis: 'Preach the Word' (2 Tim. 4:2).

Such preaching plays a central part in pastoral work, for it is the main means by which the people of God are built up in faith. John Owen, the great Puritan vice-chancellor of seventeenth-century Oxford, put it clearly: 'The first and principal duty of a pastor is to feed the flock by the diligent preaching of the Word.' Hence, the sermon is not a mere postscript to a service, nor is it to be seen as distinct from the service. It is itself part of the worship, for it is not a display of a man's talents, but a forgiven sinner's attempt in the power of the Spirit to glorify God and to stir his hearers to a like response of adoration.

If, then, preaching is to turn people to the God who is to be worshipped in spirit and in truth, it must be doctrinal in content. The so-called sermon which consists of a series of anecdotes loosely joined together by a thread of Scripture, is far removed from true preaching, which should have at its very centre the great truths of the gospel. This does not mean that each sermon must expound a particular doctrine, for some will be dealing with issues of conduct. But in every sermon the doctrinal framework must be there. Modern buildings may appear as large areas of glass, but hidden from view are the interlacings of steel girders which, like the bone structure of the body, give the buildings their stability. If the sermon is to be delivered from being the flabby homily which is often presented, it must have the hidden undergirding of biblical doctrine.

Preaching must be expository in method. It is not a case of a man speaking about God, but God using human lips to speak to men. This means that the preacher must aim, to use another Puritan phrase, 'to open up the Word'. He must not engage in imposition, in which the text of Scripture is simply the peg on which he hangs his own thoughts. His aim rather is exposition, in which he discloses to his hearers the treasure which the Spirit of God has placed within the Scriptures. Charles Simeon, whose preaching stirred eighteenth-century Cambridge, summed up the task as he saw it — to say no more and no less than was in the text before him. The preacher must prepare by listening to God as he studies the Word in order that the congregation may hear the Word which God has spoken to him, so that both he and they may worship and adore.

The preacher must keep clearly in view the glory of God through the building up of God's people. This should guard him against the snare of professionalism, which is one of the besetting sins of the preacher. He is not in the pulpit to exhibit his wisdom or his expository gifts. His sermon is not a display of his oratory or his facility in illustrating his arguments. This is not to belittle either intellectual ability or eloquence, for both play their part, but simply to keep them in their proper place as servants whose task is to draw attention, not to themselves, but to the feast the Master has provided for His guests.

The preacher will thus be more concerned to explain the Word so that people will understand, rather than to elicit their admiration for his pulpit ability. To be so plain in the manner of delivery that the humblest believer will grasp the truth will be his constant ambition, though he has to admit that at times he will fall far short. This does not of course mean that he must always remain at an elementary level. There is a place for stretching the minds of the hearers, and it is no service to a congregation to pander to the natural desire for a diet which is easily assimilated and requires little mental effort. Yet even as he compels them to think deeply, he must still aim to be plain. Some men may acquire a reputation for being deep when in fact they are simply turgid and obscure.

Constantly the preacher must remind himself that he has definite aims in view. He is not to be content with informing his hearers' minds, important as it is to convey to them the truths of Scripture. He must also aim to probe their consciences with the convicting Word, to stir their hearts to respond to the warmth of the message of grace and to move their wills to obedience to God's revealed will. Charles Simeon well summed up the aims which controlled his own ministry: 'To humble the sinner, to exalt the Saviour, and to promote holiness.'

The character and the aim of the preaching ministry will deeply influence the preacher's understanding of his work. It should also stimulate the people in their sympathetic praying for him, and in their preparation for their part on the Lord's Day. He must, in the first place, be deeply aware of his commission. He is not in the ministry — certainly he should not be — because it was a profession which appealed to him, but because he had no other option in face of the pressure of God upon his soul. Amos sums up this pressure in his reply to the worldly ecclesiastic who challenged his right to denounce the unrighteousness of the nation: 'I was neither a prophet nor a prophet's son, but I was a shepherd, and I also took care of sycamore fig-trees. But the Lord took me from tending the flock and said to me, "Go, prophesy to my people Israel."'

Then again, the faithful preacher and the receptive hearer must be persuaded of the infallible certainty of the Word of God. The preacher must begin with this, and the hearer, while he may begin with doubts, must ultimately bow in submission to the Word if he is to hear aright. A preacher who has doubts about the gospel is a menace to any congregation. The pulpit is no place for hesitant uncertainty. It is a platform from which the herald of God announces with profound conviction the truth of God's own most holy Word.

To preach is to face times of discouragement, and such a mood will inevitably affect the presentation of the message, and so will cast a shadow over the worshipping congregation. Such discouragement will not depart in face of a bout of wishful thinking. It must none the less be resisted if the preacher is to be liberated for his task. One sure weapon for combating it, and indeed for constantly reinvigorating the ministry, is a recollection of the greatness and certainty of God's plan of redemption. God is not improvising to meet each new situation. He is not devising fresh expedients as circumstances alter. He has a great plan which He had in view before the world began. That plan He is carrying forward with irrestible grace until its final consummation. It was this truth which gave Paul fresh courage as he faced the dif-

ficulties in Corinth. The task was overwhelming in a city
which was notorious for its immorality. Even the great apostle
quailed in face of the need. Then God spoke to reassure him:
'Do not be afraid; keep on speaking, do not be silent. For I
am with you, and no-one is going to attack and harm you,
because I have many people in this city' (Acts 18:10). The
people of God were lost to view in the sea of paganism of
which they were still a part. But the grace of God which had
chosen them 'before the creation of the world' (Eph. 1:4)
would surely call them. It is this assurance which lifts preaching to a new level. It is not the defiant cry of a retreating
minority, but the trumpet-call of an army which may at times
be under tremendous pressure, but which has in prospect the
assurance of total victory.

The preacher must be concerned about the needs of those
to whom he ministers. He follows a Master who wept over
Jerusalem in her impenitence. He must pray for a like concern
for those who are as yet without God and without hope. He
must also be deeply concerned for the state of the church. He
must share something of the burden which so obviously lay
on the heart of the apostle Paul, who longed so intensely for
the welfare of the churches. True preaching cannot be
divorced from the needs of the people to whom it is directed;
otherwise it becomes a mere exercise in religious theorizing.
But such application to human needs will only come from
one whose own heart is deeply stirred.

All these requirements — and how searching they are —
imply that above all else the preacher should cultivate the
intimacy of his own communion with God. It is in that
experience that he will be humbled as he discovers the pride
of his own heart, his lack of discipline, his sloth, his lack of
love. It is there, however, that he will taste the sweetness of
forgiveness and of renewed fellowship. There also he will find
himself being commissioned anew for his task, and will go to
the pulpit with a sermon which has gripped his own soul and
heart. John Owen put it so well: 'A preacher preacheth that
sermon only well unto others which preacheth itself in his
own soul.' To go from such communion with God, and then
to find a congregation who themselves have prepared in spirit
to receive the Word — this is a sure prelude to a time of worship when Christ will be exalted, His gospel vindicated and

the glory of the Lord will fill the house.

The hearers

It is right that the highest standards should be set for the preaching of the Word of God. The preacher should set his sights on the target of being what Paul describes as 'a workman who does not need to be ashamed and who correctly handles the word of truth' (2 Tim. 2:15). The congregation has a right to expect from the man who summons them to obedience to the Word, a like commitment on his part. What is, however, not always remembered, is that the preacher also has a right to expect from a worshipping congregation a readiness to give themselves to the exacting work of listening to the preaching with full concentration of all their powers. The great preacher, the Lord Jesus Christ Himself, certainly insisted on this commitment by His hearers. So He confronted them with His firm requirement that they should pay careful attention to the message which was preached.

This command, to which reference was made earlier in this chapter in the context of active participation by the hearers, comes in two forms. Mark gives as his version of the Lord's saying: 'Consider carefully what you hear' (Mark 4:24) while Luke recalls the words: 'Consider carefully how you listen' (Luke 8:18). The variation between the two evangelists serves, however, to give us complementary aspects of the Lord's command. We are to concentrate on the content of the message so that we may assimilate and so profit from it. This in turn requires that we should pay heed to the conditions which we must fulfil in order to achieve such concentration.

The context of the saying is the parable of the sower. In this case the constant factors were the activity of the sower and the quality of the seed. The variable factor was the nature of the soil. So, in the application, the Lord who sows the seed remains constant in His work, and the Word of God which He sows has the same unchanging excellence whenever and wherever it is preached. What varies is the specific human response, whether it is the total neglect of the Word, the shallow emotional but temporary acceptance, the reception which is soon choked by other issues, or the fruitful response of the believing and obedient hearer. It was in this context that the

Lord reinforced the application of His parable by underlining the need for a right hearing of the Word.

He further emphasized the point by drawing out the implications of our response: 'Whoever has will be given more; whoever does not have, even what he thinks he has will be taken from him' (Luke 8:18). His message is clear: we shall be paid back in our own measure. If we receive and assimilate the truth, it will qualify us to receive further truth. If, on the other hand, we fail to give heed to the truth declared to us, we will lose even what we already seem to have. So, our response to preaching is either progressively beneficial or correspondingly injurious. There is no such thing as neutrality in face of the Word of God. We cannot switch off mentally and detach ourselves from the scrutiny of the message. Either we hear it with profit and so fit ourselves to hear more and to profit more, or else we do not receive the Word and as a result not only forfeit the blessing of God, but also disqualify ourselves from further fruitful hearing.

J. C. Ryle in his *Expository Thoughts on Luke* commented with his usual forcefulness: 'The degree of benefit which men receive from all the means of grace depends entirely on the way in which they use them. Private prayer lies at the very foundation of religion; yet the mere formal repetition of a set of words when the heart is far away does good to no man's soul. Reading the Bible is essential to the attainment of sound Christian knowledge; yet the mere formal reading of so many chapters as a task or duty, without a humble desire to be taught of God, is little better than a waste of time. Just as it is with praying or Bible reading, so it is with hearing. It is not enough that we go to church and hear sermons. We may do so for fifty years, and be "nothing bettered, but rather worse". "Take heed," says our Lord, "how you hear."'

A preacher who is true to his commission is subject to the sovereign direction of the Spirit of God. This means that he must make every endeavour to present the message faithfully. To adulterate the gospel, or to adapt it in order to please some or to avoid offending others, is one of the worst crimes he can commit. He must not alter or manipulate the message for it is the Word of God which has been entrusted to him. But the hearer is under a like constraint. Yet often those who hear change the message to their own great spiritual loss.

They may shut their minds to its searching requirements in the way described by Matthew: 'This people's heart has become calloused; they hardly hear with their ears, and they have closed their eyes. Otherwise they might see with their eyes, hear with their ears, understand with their hearts and turn, and I would heal them' (Matt. 13:15). Then again, the hearer may apply the Word to someone else — the attitude of the Pharisee to the tax collector in Jesus' parable is a favourite reaction of a troubled conscience which looks for another object for the words of judgement. A further way of evading the Word is to try and adapt it in such a way that it no longer cuts incisively into our own comfortable existence. The bright light of the sun may appear coloured as it shines through stained glass, but that tint is not its true radiance. The light of truth may likewise be modified within our minds and hearts by the filter of our own wisdom or our own selfishness, but the truth remains essentially the same and will expose us fully on the Day of Judgement when all evasion will finally cease.

How then shall we ensure that we hear in the right way? Ryle gives three basic requirements — that we hear with faith, with reverence and with prayer. We will certainly not profit from the Word of God if there is what the writer to the Hebrews describes as 'a sinful, unbelieving heart' (Heb. 3:12). Such unbelief cancels the impact of the Word. Thus the writer continues in the same vein as he recalls Israel's failure: 'The message they heard was of no value to them, because those who heard did not combine it with faith' (Heb. 4:2). A believing approach is also a reverent approach. The Thessalonians profited from Paul's preaching because they 'accepted it not as the word of men, but as it actually is, the word of God' (1 Thess. 2:13). Such an acceptance of the Word implies a spirit of prayer. The prayer of the psalmist is always appropriate: 'Open my eyes that I may see wonderful things in your law' (Ps. 119:18). So too is the prayer of Samuel: 'Speak, for your servant is listening' (1 Sam. 3:10).

Hearing the Word is obviously in the first place an action of the mind. The preacher is communicating the truth of God, and doing so by means of intelligible words and rational argument. The first response is therefore an attempt to grasp the essential content of the message. The prophetic call: '"Come now, let us reason together," says the Lord' (Isa. 1:18) might well be the prelude to every sermon. So we must apply our minds to the content of the word which is being preached. This requires a determined and sustained effort. 'The birds of the air' in the parable are constantly in flight every time the Word is faithfully presented. The devil will use anything — from wandering thoughts, the sound of traffic outside, the flaking of the paintwork behind the pulpit — anything to distract our minds. So we must concentrate.

That is why listening to preaching is a demanding exercise. I recall someone who sat under the ministry of Dr Lloyd-Jones at Westminster Chapel. She told him on one occasion that she felt mentally quite exhausted after the sustained expositions from the pulpit. Far from encouraging any tendency to self-pity, he was insistent that in fact she should expect to be stretched by the preaching. After all, to hear a sermon is not to engage in a leisure activity but to discipline our minds so that, with all our mental powers at full stretch, we might aim to grasp all that God has to say to us on each occasion.

Such mental activity will not cease after the sermon is over. The word will be recalled and the personal application will be developed. The word 'ruminate' is appropriate here. It is allied with the noun 'ruminant' which is the name for that group of animals which chew the cud, and so complete the process of digesting the food which they have already eaten. So, too, we ruminate on the message we have heard when we bring it back to mind, chew over it and draw from it further nourishment for our souls.

Hearing the Word of God must, of course, go beyond mental apprehension for the preaching is directed not only to our intellect but to our conscience. It is the voice of a holy God spoken to sinners. That is why it comes at times with such a stinging rebuke and with such humbling power. To try and hide from God, like Adam in the trees of the garden, is a futile exercise before the omniscient One who searches us out. To try and conceal our guilt, like Achan with his loot buried in the tent, is equally pointless. Profitable hearing of the Word is closely wedded to the prayer: 'Search me, O God, and know my heart; test me and know my anxious thoughts. See if there is any offensive way in me, and lead me in the way everlasting' (Ps. 139:23-24).

To hear in this way is to be ready to submit to whatever demands the Word makes on us. In the parable of the sower the fruitful response is one which springs from those 'who hear the word, retain it, and by persevering, produce a crop' (Luke 8:15). That crop is detailed by Paul as he describes the fruit of the Spirit, seen in the quality of a consistently righteous life (Gal. 5:22-23). He himself had reacted to his first encounter with Christ on the Damascus road with a question which remained the characteristic attitude of the rest of his life: 'What shall I do, Lord?' (Acts 22:10.)

Submission to the Word must not be construed in any legalistic way. A feet-dragging conformity to demands reluctantly accepted is certainly not the biblical pattern. When the Lord confronts us with His Word, he does not look for a dutiful compliance. Rather, He requires glad and whole-hearted submission by a disciple who has caught some glimpse of the perfect obedience of Jesus Himself reflected in the words of the psalmist applied to the Lord in the Epistle to the Hebrews: 'Here I am, I have come to do your will, O God' (Heb. 10:7,9). It is not enough simply to hear the Word. Jesus himself added the necessary qualification which makes the hearing profitable: 'Blessed . . . are those who hear the word of God and obey it' (Luke 11:28).

6 *Now about the collection!*

The incentive

Christian giving is not merely a response to the need of finance to support the work of the churches or of missions. An emotional appeal for funds, in which pressure is put on people by virtue of particular needs, is not the primary approach. The minister of the gospel must not be reduced to the level of a fund-raiser, nor must the missionary be forced into the role of the Buddhist monk with his begging bowl. Christian giving is indeed a responsibility, but it is also a privilege. It is demanded by the needs which confront us but is even more insistently required by God. There are, of course, needs to be met and such needs must be presented to us so that we may know in what direction to channel our gifts. But there is an even more fundamental reason for giving. It is because God has commanded it.

Man's basic responsibility is to glorify God. The word from Deuteronomy 6:13 which Jesus quoted in His reply to Satan (Luke 4:8) has a positive emphasis: 'Worship the Lord your God and serve him only.' Jesus Himself in His high-priestly prayer summed up His own supreme achievement: 'I have brought you glory on earth' (John 17:4). For Him, to glorify God was the climax of all human service. God is Himself glorious both in the perfection of His nature, and in the display of that perfection in His works of creation, providence and redemption. We glorify Him when by our words and deeds we declare to men and to angels, and above all to God Himself, how great and good and loving He is.

Giving, in the Bible, is rooted in this basic requirement to worship God — a requirement which is no legal burden to the Christian, but which elicits rather the glad response of a grateful heart. So one of the words of wisdom from the book of Proverbs is the command: 'Honour the Lord with your wealth'

(Prov. 3:9). A child honours his parents when he respects them, acknowledges their authority, and shows his respect in a practical way by obedience. So the Christian honours God, not only with the praise of his lips in which he acknowledges with reverence the glory of his Creator, but also as he brings his money as a willing offering.

To worship with our money is to acknowledge that He is the source of the money we give, and indeed of our willingness to give it! He is our Creator and has filled the earth with the good things which we so enjoy. He has created us with our distinctive skills and abilities so that our earnings are the evidence, not of some innate ability for which we can take credit, but of the wisdom of God who created us in such a way that we can earn our livelihood.

By His providence He has placed us in a certain nation and a particular family; He has seen to it that we have had a particular education and acquired a certain training or qualification; He has directed our steps to the job we occupy and the income we enjoy. So our giving is a token of our recognition of the providence of God which has led us and provided for us, and also a practical way of honouring Him for the love and wisdom and power which are reflected in His providential dealings with us.

There is, however, a further incentive as we aim to honour God with our money. While we owe our very life to our Creator, and while we recognize in our present circumstances the providence of God, we have an even greater debt, for He who made us has also redeemed us by the blood of His Son. If we are stirred to wonder by the majesty of creation and if we are moved to gratitude by the providential ordering of our lives, then we are overwhelmed by the amazing grace of our God in sending His Son to die for us. After all, we had despised His gifts in creation, for we had used them for our own selfish ends without glorifying the Giver, as Paul so clearly points out in Romans 1. We had been blind to God's providence, attributing our good fortune or our bad luck, as we would have termed them, to a mixture of chance and our own native abilities. Yet, in spite of our blindness and our sinful ingratitude, God sent His Son to die for sinners and to deliver us from our present lost state, and from eternal misery.

It is this unbelievable grace which is to the apostle Paul the supreme incentive to us to give generously. 'You know the grace of our Lord Jesus Christ, that though he was rich, yet for your sakes he became poor, so that you through his poverty might become rich' (2 Cor. 8:9). To be gripped by the wonder of His willing impoverishment is to encounter the most powerful argument to persuade us, if we need persuading, how readily we ought to give. We cannot consider Calvary and, at the same time, lay down qualifications about our own giving. We cannot be grudging or reluctant and still sing with sincerity:

> Love so amazing, so divine,
> Demands my life, my soul, my all.

Paul disclosed the ultimate source of Christian giving as he describes the response of some of the Greek churches: 'We want you to know about the grace that God has given the Macedonian churches' (2 Cor. 8:1). He goes on to speak in detail of the characteristics of their giving but, first, he must mention the source of it all — the grace of God. Men are by nature selfish. That is why the world — or the church when it is acting like the world — has to employ high-pressure appeals buttressed by commercial techniques or gimmicks or some kind of self-interest, if money is to be raised. If such naturally self-centred people are to become willing and sacrificial givers, the grace of God must change their hearts — and, incidentally, if someone remains essentially tight-fisted, he may question whether he has really experienced the grace of God, no matter how loud his profession may be! Christian giving is neither a burdensome duty nor an emotional response to an appeal on behalf of some worthy cause. It is rather the overflow of a joyful stream whose perennial source of supply is the grace of God.

The purpose

Giving is closely linked to worship, not only in its basic character as being itself an act of worship, but in its practical importance in maintaining those whom God has appointed to lead His people in worship. In the Old Testament the Levites were set apart for the service of the sanctuary and were excluded from the apportionment of land given to the other tribes. As a result, their maintenance was a primary charge upon Israel's giving and to neglect their support was a sin

(Deut. 12:19; 18:1). The strictures of Malachi in face of the neglect of the tithe are directed to this very matter. When God calls for the tithes to be brought in and when He promises revival the aim in view is 'that there may be food in my house' (Mal. 3:10). This obviously covered both the support of the Levites and the provision of all that was needed for the sacrificial offerings. To neglect this responsibility was not merely to deprive the Levites of their due reward for their services; it was far more serious, for it meant robbing God Himself (Mal. 3:8-9).

The pattern does not change in the New Testament. When Jesus sends His disciples out to preach He lays down the principle that, 'The worker deserves his wages' (Luke 10:7). They are therefore to accept hospitality as a return for their preaching. This word of Jesus is quoted by Paul in 1 Timothy 5:18 to enforce his argument that the elders who rule the church, and especially those whose work is preaching and teaching, are 'worthy of double honour'. It is clear that this phrase refers to financial and material remuneration, for Paul quotes not only the saying of Jesus, but the law of Deuteronomy: 'Do not muzzle the ox while it is treading out the corn' (Deut. 25:4).

This same quotation from the law is also used in 1 Corinthians 9 in his firm assertion of his own right to be maintained. 'Is it about oxen that God is concerned?' he asks the Corinthians. 'Surely', he replies, 'God says this for us, doesn't he?' He argues that just as the ploughman and the harvester expect to share in the harvest which their toil has helped to bring in, so those who sow the spiritual seed of the Word of God have a right to expect 'a material harvest' from those to whom they minister. Paul makes the same point to the Galatians: 'Anyone who receives instruction in the word must share all good things with his instructor' (Gal. 6:6). Paul did not interpret these rights in some legalistic fashion and in fact, because of the peculiar problems at Corinth, he was prepared to forego his rights. But that did not mean making any concession as to the rights themselves.

One sees the same emphasis in his letter to Titus where he urges that Zenas and Apollos receive adequate provision: 'See that they have everything they need' (Titus 3:13). This care, not only for the elders of the local church, but for the itinerant preachers, is reflected in a negative way in the warning of John about a false preacher: 'Do not take him into your house or welcome him' (2 John 10). The implication is clear, that if he were a true preacher a welcome and provision would be normal.

Such giving is not viewed as a kind of statutory obligation necessitated by the practical needs of the pastor. When Paul speaks of the support he received from the Philippian church he uses the language of Old Testament worship. Their gifts for his support were 'a fragrant offering, an acceptable sacrifice, pleasing to God' (Phil. 4:18). To give money to support the ministry of the local church or the missionary of the gospel is not merely to deal with a practical necessity; it is rather to engage in an act of worship. Such giving is indeed described as a sacrifice in the Epistle to the Hebrews: 'And do not forget to do good and to share with others, for with such sacrifices God is pleased' (Heb. 13:16).

The second major charge on the giving of believers is the poor. In the Old Testament the law had a special concern for the widow and orphan, and also for the landless foreigner. When the harvest field was reaped the gleaning was not to be so thorough that the widow could not come behind the gleaners to find a share for herself. The fruit trees were not to be picked so completely that the needy would be unable to find fruit.

This tradition is carried on into the New Testament. In the early chapters of Acts there was a deep and practical concern for the needy members of the church. Indeed the sad dispute between the Greek and Aramaic-speaking Jews arose from the problem of allocating relief to the widows. The Epistles maintain the same attitude of concern: 'Let us do good to all people, especially to those who belong to the family of believers' (Gal. 6:10). 'Religion that God our Father accepts as pure and faultless is this: to look after orphans and widows in their distress' (James 1:27). 'Give proper recognition to those widows who are really in need' (1 Tim. 5:3).

Today in the industrially developed countries the growth of state welfare has altered the situation, in that material provision is made to avoid the old abject poverty of the orphan and the widow. There are, however, still needs to be met even within the welfare state. At the same time the world has contracted as far as communication is concerned. We are more vividly aware of the widows and orphans and poor of the third world. Our forefathers read about them, while we see them on television screens. The demands of the needy have not therefore lessened. Nor is the response to those needs simply a work of common compassion. It is certainly that, but it is raised to a higher level in Scripture. To assist the poor is to engage in worship. Paul puts it very strongly. To fail to do so is to mock God (Gal. 6:7 ff.). Clearly then, to comply with the demands by giving freely is not only to alleviate suffering but is to honour and glorify God.

The method

It is a great help in considering an area of Christian conduct if we have both teaching and illustration. In the matter of 'how we give' this is exactly what Paul provides in 2 Corinthians 8 and 9, though it is in the reverse order, for he first illustrates the kind of giving which he wants to see, and then he applies the illustration to their own responsibility. His illustration is not drawn from his imagination but from a real live situation. So he quotes the generous giving of the Macedonian churches as an example of how Christians ought to give to the Lord.

Their giving was in the first place independent of their circumstances. They did not take the rather natural attitude of assessing their own resources and likely personal demands, before giving a fraction of their money to God. Their approach was in fact quite the reverse, for they gave out of all proportion to their ability. They had been going through great trouble. This probably meant persecution which in turn produced hardship. In a situation where membership of a trade guild was necessary if a man was to ply his trade, expulsion meant the loss of his livelihood and grinding poverty for him and his family.

Such a condition may lead either to self-pity or to a dogged persistence. But in fact the Macedonians displayed a truly Christian reaction in that they rejoiced at their trials and their poverty. Such indeed was the depth of their joy that it overflowed in generous giving. To the early believers, suffering was God's gift to them — the disciples for example left the council at Jerusalem after their beating, rejoicing that they had been counted worthy to suffer for Christ (Acts 5:41).

So here, these Macedonians did not consider that their poverty excused them from giving. On the contrary they felt that God had honoured them by calling on them to suffer and they must therefore repay His favour to them by their giving.

At the heart of their giving Paul sees the ultimate reason for their generosity: 'They gave themselves first to the Lord' (2 Cor. 8:5). Because the matter of supreme concern to them was their personal relationship with the Lord, their giving was lifted to a different level from that of mere duty. They loved the Lord because He had first loved them. They were grateful to Him because of His goodness to them. The conclusion they drew was not a mere logical deduction but was the warm response of their hearts. So they gave themselves in utter submission to Him and looked around for practical ways to show their love. Like a husband deeply in love with his wife who brings gifts, not because he thinks it is what is required of husbands, but because of his affection for her, so they gave to the Lord, not out of duty, but because they loved Him. Christian giving is essentially a love gift to the Lord who has saved us.

They gave systematically 'as much as they were able' (2 Cor. 8:3). This is a principle which Paul laid down in his first letter to the Corinthians: 'On the first day of every week, each one of you should set aside a sum of money in keeping with his income' (1 Cor. 16:2). Our giving is not to be sporadic, with an ebb or flow dictated by our moods or by some pressing need. We should lay aside from our income in a systematic way the money to be given to the Lord.

This principle of systematic giving is rooted in the Old Testament practice of giving a tenth as a basic offering to God. Tithing was not in the first place one of the regulations of the law of Moses. The Mosaic legislation simply embodied what was already a long-established practice. Abraham gave tithes to Melchizedek and clearly it was because the latter was 'the priest of God Most High' (Gen. 14:18). Abraham's gift of 'a tenth of everything' was an expression of gratitude to God for his recent deliverance.

It is this element of gratitude which is also prominent in Jacob's vow at Bethel. Although the hoped-for protection and provision are still in the future he anticipates them, and as a token of his thanksgiving for these expected mercies he makes his promise to God: 'Of all that you give me I will give you a tenth' (Gen. 28:22).

The law of Moses takes this existing practice and gives detailed regulations for its observance, and at the same time emphasizes the gratitude from which tithing should spring, and which elevates it from being a mere legal device. Thus in the law of Deuteronomy the Israelite is to preface his offerings with a recital before the priest of all God's goodness (Deut. 26:1-11). The tithe, however, was not an optional extra. It was holy and as such belonged to the Lord (Lev. 27:30,32). To withhold it was therefore to be guilty of theft, a crime particularly serious in this context as it involved God (Mal. 3:8-9).

There is obviously no legal requirement in the New Testament that we give a tenth of our income. At the same time the age-old principle is still a great help in promoting disciplined giving. It is only too easy to talk piously of exercising Christian liberty in our giving when we may simply be covering our own inadequate response with a veneer of pseudo-spirituality. The tenth is a good basic guide-line and to this we may add other free-will offerings as God's Spirit prompts us. The pattern for this is in the Old Testament where a believer would donate to the Lord a special thank offering in addition to his normal obligations.

The Macedonians certainly did not stop at a basic level. Their giving was sacrificial. They did not give a proportion which left them with a generous allowance for themselves. They gave 'beyond their ability' (2 Cor. 8:3). One recalls the Lord's commendation of the poor widow whose temple offering seemed so pitifully small, compared with the large donations of the more affluent members. Yet hers, in Jesus' view, was the largest offering. The others had given out of their wealth and had plenty left over, whereas she had given everything she had. The measure of sacrificial giving is not the amount given but the amount left behind!

A further feature of their giving was its spontaneity. Theirs was an 'overflowing joy' which together with their extreme poverty 'welled up in rich generosity' (8:2). No one pushed them into giving. Indeed they did it 'entirely on their own' (8:3). Such in fact was the exuberance of their spontaneous generosity that they 'urgently pleaded' (8:4) that they might have the privilege of sharing in the fund being raised to help the Christians in Judea. Here is the exact opposite of the situation which all too often prevails today, when appeals are directed to potential donors. In this case it was the donors who were clamouring for the opportunity of contributing, and doing so with an urgency which brooked no refusal.

This brief glimpse of generous giving is a powerful argument as Paul applies the lessons to the Corinthians. Since, however, this is God-given Scripture, the application is an abiding one and the principles apply to twentieth-century Christians just as much as they did to the believers of the first century. This systematic, sacrificial and spontaneous giving, rooted as it was in loving devotion to the Lord, is not presented as an interesting cameo of a group of churches in Greece, but as a stimulus provided by the Holy Spirit to spur us to a like generosity. So Paul applies the Macedonian illustration to the Corinthian situation — and also to ours!

He rejoices that already there is evidence of a right attitude, but he is concerned that their intentions are carried out. It is fatally easy to intend to do many things which because of our indolence or indiscipline remain undone. We may be stirred by the story of some generous giving. We may be moved by a sermon or an article on the subject. Yet our generous intentions may peter out into a very inadequate response to the needs which cry out for help. So he urges them, 'Now finish the work, so that your eager willingness to do it may be matched by your completion of it' (8:11).

His great desire is that their giving should have the element of spontaneity. So he rejoices as he sees their 'eagerness to help'. They are, he acknowledges, 'ready to help' and this 'enthusiasm' (9:2) is a delight to him. But it has been even more valuable for, as often happens, enthusiasm is infectious, and the zeal of Achaia had stirred others. When some Christians in a local church begin to see their responsibilities, and when they become enthusiastic givers, often there is a congregational impact, and a sluggish and dutifully giving church becomes a generous supporter of the work of God at home and overseas.

This stress on spontaneous liberality is brought out by a negative and also a positive argument. There are certain factors which should not be present in Christian giving and certain features which should characterize it. Turning first to the negatives, we find Paul insisting that money should not be 'grudgingly given' (9:5). The Authorized Version brings out the literal meaning of the Greek, which is that our giving is not to be 'as from covetousness'. The latter is viewed in Scripture as a particularly pernicious sin. Jesus warned His disciples to beware of it and told the parable of the rich fool to illustrate the point (Luke 12:15-21). Paul puts it in the same category as immorality (Eph. 5:3) and idolatry (Col. 3:5). It is the grasping attitude which greedily acquires, but very unwillingly relinquishes what has been gained. Such an unreadiness, reflected as it is in a merely dutiful giving, is totally unacceptable.

There are two more negatives which reinforce the argument. We must not give 'reluctantly' (2 Cor. 9:7). Again the Greek is vivid — 'not out of grief'. Here is a man who parts with his money so reluctantly that it evidently pains him to give. The other phrase simply supplements the picture, speaking as it does of giving 'from necessity' or 'under compulsion'. Such giving is clearly painful to the giver and is no pleasure to the Lord.

On the positive side the gift is to be a generous one (9:5). The word used here is one also used in Scripture of God's bounty to us. So the generosity of which Paul speaks is one which reflects the overflowing liberality of the great Giver Himself. Such readiness is highlighted by the other positive word Paul uses: 'God loves a cheerful giver' (9:7). The Greek word here translated 'cheerful' appears in our English word 'hilarious'. We all know what a hilarious occasion is like! It is one where spontaneous delight is expressed in an uninhibited way, with a blend of fun and laughter and sheer delight. To speak of a hilarious giver is clearly to envisage a Christian who is poles apart from the dutiful contributor to church funds or to a missionary offering.

Paul sums up the attitude in another word which may be translated 'to excel' or 'to abound'. The Macedonian Christians had excelled in their giving (8:7) and Paul wants this to be the general pattern (9:8). The Christian is not to aim at the minimum standard in the realm of giving. He is not to ask: 'How much do I have to give?' for this is really a veiled way of asking: 'How little is an acceptable offering?' He is rather to be like a keen examination candidate whose aim is not the pass level but distinction. He wants to excel in his giving, not to impress others, for in fact his giving will be known only to himself and to the Lord, but in order to display to God his abounding gratitude.

Paul sees further fruitful consequences. It is not only that the giver shows his own gratitude to God by his gift; he enables those who benefit from his gift to thank God in their turn. Indeed the measure of prosperity God gives him is not to be seen as a reward for his own generous giving but as a provision to enable him to give all the more so that more and more will benefit and thanksgiving to God will correspondingly increase.

The argument comes full circle. It begins with the grace of God which gives so generously that it elicits joyful gratitude. This attitude of thankfulness results in worship which is expressed in spontaneous and generous giving. This in turn leads to further thanksgiving, this time on the part of those who have benefited from the gift. Those who gave have been prospered by God, and having learnt already how to give they simply give all the more. This again leads to a wider circle of those who share in the gifts and so to a swelling volume of praise to God. The whole process lifts the mind and the heart to the source of it all: 'Thanks be to God for his indescribable gift' (9:15). We are back where we began with the grace of God which gave the greatest gift of all, even Christ, and with Him has freely given us all things.

7 Baptism

The visible word

Christ not only gave His disciples a message to preach, but
instituted also for His people two outward observances which
were to be continued in the life of the church. It was characteristic of the Lord in His teaching ministry to use ordinary
people or events to convey spiritual truth. Thus He pointed
to a man sowing seed, to a fisherman pulling his nets to land,
to a building being erected, to a vine being pruned. It is therefore consistent with His general teaching pattern that He
should take two very ordinary human actions − taking a bath
and having a meal − and use them as outward signs of the
blessings of the gospel. Washing our bodies to remove dirt
and nourishing our bodies with food and drink are basic to
normal life. Here then is the background for the two signs
which speak of our cleansing from sin and our strengthening
for serving God.

Rome has added to the list and claims that there are seven
sacraments. The Thirty-Nine Articles of the Church of England
well reject this notion. Some of these, like penance or extreme
unction, are the result of a corruption of apostolic teaching.
Others, like marriage or ordination, are allowed in the Scripture, 'but yet' comments Article 25, 'have not like nature of
Sacraments with Baptism and the Lord's Supper for that they
have not any visible sign or ceremony ordained by Christ'.
Basic therefore to the two gospel sacraments is the fact that
the Lord Jesus Himself ordained them and by word and
action specified the elements which should be used, namely
water, bread and wine, and the words which should accompany them. These observances are, however, not mere empty
ceremonies. They are significant and point to the blessings of
the gospel. The Shorter Catechism sums up their meaning in
its usual succinct fashion: 'A sacrament is an holy ordinance

instituted by Christ; wherein by sensible signs, Christ, and the benefits of the new covenant are represented, sealed, and applied to believers.'

The institution of both ordinances came at significant moments. The Lord's supper was instituted the very night when Jesus was betrayed and was thus intimately linked with His death. The command to baptize was part of His final commission to His disciples in which evangelism, baptism and teaching are closely tied together. The disciples clearly understood their commission, for on the first great preaching occasion recorded in Acts 2 there is a complete conformity to it. The gospel preaching leads to the enquiry of the convicted hearers, the command to be baptized to their submission, and the teaching given to the converts to the breaking of bread. There was thus no hiatus between Word and ordinance, for both were bound together in the total preaching and in the people's response.

It is possible to reduce both baptism and the Lord's supper to mere badges or distinguishing marks of a Christian's profession. They are, however, much more than outward tokens of membership in the church of Christ. It is true that in baptism a man declares his faith in Christ, and in the supper he affirms his communion with the Lord, and with his fellow Christians. To deny the importance of this profession of faith would be to run contrary to the tenor of Scripture. The question, however, is not whether this outward profession of faith is essential, but whether it is the only or even the major element in the ordinances. Are they, in short, services in which I say something to God or, rather, in which God says something to me and to which I respond? Am I taking the initiative in committing myself to the Lord, or am I simply responding to the overtures of His grace? We are really asking the most basic question: is salvation by grace alone? The answer of Scripture is an unequivocal 'Yes'!

The inadequate view, which makes a man's profession of faith primary, springs from even deeper roots of error. It is embedded in the false premise, itself the product of human pride, which makes man the primary focus of attention rather than God. So man speculates and forms his religious theories as he reaches out towards the unknown God. Man struggles to understand himself and to master his moral failures, and

God joins with him in the conflict. Man gropes after a knowledge of God and devises means of worship which meet his
needs. God as a result ceases to be the almighty Lord of
Scripture, and is reduced to a shadowy projection of man's
own thinking, a product of the religious imagination, a deity
made in man's image and after his likeness. Instead of the
sovereign God who initiates and carries out the work of salvation, we have a rather tentative deity who waits hopefully
for man to provide him with an opportunity to give the
additional help required. Such an understanding of the way
of salvation may not be expressed in such an explicit way.
Indeed it may be rejected, at least in theory. Yet it often
lurks in the background and colours the thinking even of
Christians. The old heresy of Pelagius, which virtually made
man his own saviour, may still reappear in an adulterated
semi-Pelagian form. The net result is the same. Human pride
does not relinquish its hold on the heart of sinful men.

The Bible, by contrast, begins not with man but with God.
Whether in creation, providence or redemption, God is the
initiator, the controller and the director, whereas man is
always the recipient, the listener and the respondent. Thus
the basic presupposition of Scripture is that there is one true
living God who is independent of men. This God has not
remained silent but has spoken. He has revealed Himself in
His great deeds in history. Nor has He left men to try and
interpret these deeds, for in the prophetic and apostolic
testimonies He has added to His actions His own explanation
of their significance. This process of revelation has reached its
climax in the Incarnation, for Jesus Christ, the Son of the
living God, is Himself the Word, the final and complete statement of God Almighty. Man's task, therefore, is not to reflect
on ultimate issues and then to try and express these reflections in some form of worship; it is rather to listen to what
God has spoken, and to submit to the guidance of God's Spirit
who alone is able to enlighten men to understand God's Word.

The Reformation of the sixteenth century was such a radical movement because it revolutionized Christian thinking by
driving the Reformers from their man-centred thinking to a
God-orientated one. Their great aim was to listen to the voice
of the sovereign God whose words they heard in the Bible, as
the Holy Spirit applied its message to their minds and hearts.

This affected their view of preaching which now became a primary means of grace, in that it was a gracious proclamation of the Word of God. It also affected their view of baptism and the Lord's supper. These were no longer seen as primarily the actions of men, but in the first place as the declarations of God.

The phrase that sums up their conviction is the description of the ordinances of the gospel as 'the Visible Words'. The descriptive title was taken from Augustine, the great fifth-century theologian, and very aptly describes their nature and purpose. When the Word is preached it is the audible word and the congregation listens. When baptism is administered and the Lord's supper is celebrated that same Word is preached by visual means. They are the divinely given visual aids to drive home the message declared from the pulpit. Cranmer put it well in his *Treatise on the Lord's Supper:* 'Our Saviour Christ . . . hath ordained one visible sacrament of spiritual regeneration in water, and another visible sacrament of spiritual nourishment in bread and wine, to the intent, that as much as it is possible for man, we may see Christ with our eyes, smell him at our nose, taste him with our mouths, grope with him with our hands, and perceive him with all our senses. For as the word of God preached putteth Christ into our ears, so likewise these elements of water, bread, and wine, joined to God's word, do after a sacramental manner put Christ into our eyes, mouths, hands, and all our senses.'[1]

When the 'audible word' is preached Christ meets with men and women and speaks to them. From one point of view words are spoken by human lips and heard with human ears, just as they are in any verbal interchange. But in preaching there is something more than a man's speech and a hearer's intelligent grasp of what is said. In a way beyond our defining Christ accompanies the preached word into the heart of the hearer. So a man may recall a sermon in purely human terms as he mentions the name of the preacher to whom he listened. But he may also recall it as a vivid spiritual encounter with God. So he says, 'Christ spoke to me.' He may also say, 'Christ came to me in power.' Both statements are true for

1. Cranmer: *Selected Writings,* Ed. C. S. Meyers, S.P.C.K., London, 1961, p. 56.

the Lord accompanies His Word and uses it as the key to open our hearts.

This implies, of course, a response on the hearer's part. He not only listens to the preaching but applies his mind to understand it. He assesses it in the light of Scripture, just as the Bereans tested the preaching of Paul by the criterion of the Old Testament. By God's grace he accepts it as God's word to his own soul, and in humble obedience he applies it to his own life. To listen to a sermon is thus not a mere exercise in mental concentration; it is an experience of spiritual involvement with the preacher in order that the audible word from the pulpit may be the Lord's own word to a receptive heart.

In the same way, the visible word is a declaration of the gospel. It does not say something different from the audible word. It does not have some special message. A good visual aid in a children's meeting does not add a new element to the address — if it does it is a bad visual aid, or is badly employed! A good visual aid rather reinforces, by its appeal to the eyes, what the spoken word is saying to the ears. So the word displayed visibly in baptism and the Lord's supper is the same word as is preached from the pulpit. Different means of communication are employed but the essential content of the message remains the same since, in both the audible and the visible words, Christ is proclaimed. In both cases the response is the same — the Word is received by faith.

Common to the effective ministry both of the audible and visible words is the activity of the Holy Spirit. When the Word is preached the aim of the preacher should be that his ministry might be 'with a demonstration of the Spirit's power' (1 Cor. 2:4) and at the same time his prayer will be that the Spirit will be at work in those who hear. It is through this activity of the Spirit both in preacher and congregation that the proclamation of the grace of God meets the answering response of faith. The Spirit opens the mind to grasp the meaning of the gospel, probes the conscience to feel the deep pain of conviction, stirs the heart to feel the loathsomeness of sin in face of the holiness of God and moves the will so that the penitent sinner turns to embrace the offered mercy.

Since the visible word is a proclamation of the same gospel, the activity of the Holy Spirit is equally necessary. The

Scriptures have no time for a Roman view of the sacraments where the due performance, assuming the correct form and material elements are used, leads to the communication of the blessing. What is needed is the accompanying work of the Holy Spirit, who with His life-giving power presents Christ to the recipient of the ordinance, and grants the gift of faith to receive the Word.

The Christian life begins in a supernatural work of grace. The new birth is a miracle effected by the power of the Holy Spirit and without that spiritual rebirth there is no Christian experience. This is why Jesus confronted Nicodemus at the outset with the necessity of being born again. It is out of this work of the Spirit that faith is born. 'No-one can say, "Jesus is Lord," except by the Holy Spirit' (1 Cor. 12:3). Faith is the first cry of the new-born child of God, directed with confidence to a gracious Saviour.

A word of assurance

The summons of the gospel is not to a tentative faith in which confidence and doubt jostle together for mastery in the soul. The goal rather is a well-grounded faith, which is closely linked with assurance. So John in his first letter sets out his aim in penning his message to them: 'I write these things to you who believe in the name of the Son of God so that you may know that you have eternal life' (1 John 5:13). There is, of course, a false assurance based on a mere outward profession, and this John rejects as sinful presumption. The alternative to this, however, is not a continuing state of uncertainty, in which there is an uneasy equilibrium between hope and despair. It is rather a deep and abiding conviction that the great change has not been a piece of religious wishful thinking, but a true saving work of Christ.

It is the Spirit who gives this inner assurance. He is the Spirit of sonship who 'testifies with our spirit that we are God's children' (Rom. 8:16). He is the powerful Witness who authenticates our stammering profession of faith and answers both the doubts of our own hearts and the accusations of Satan with the reassuring word of divine acceptance. The Spirit gives this inner assurance by testifying directly to our spirit, but he also uses the instrumentality of the Word of God. It is His use of Scripture which lifts us from the level of a mere self-persuasion. It is not that we try by a mental effort to appropriate promises from the Bible and apply them to ourselves. Rather it is a case of the Spirit taking those promises and assuring us that we may lay claim to their efficacy for us.

It is in this ministry to the new-born Christian that we see the role which baptism plays. It is associated in the New Testament with the beginning of the Christian life, whereas the Lord's supper is linked with the ongoing development of the believer's experience. This is seen in the fact that baptism is a once-for-all ordinance, while the Lord's supper is regularly observed right through our life. Then again the practice in the Acts of the Apostles of baptizing converts as soon as they profess faith, even on a desert road or at midnight, identifies a man's conversion and his baptism very closely. It is thus the initial word which the Spirit speaks to the regenerate soul, and as such is in the first place an assurance of acceptance.

This is brought out in Paul's references to baptism in Romans 6 and Colossians 2 where it is seen to be declaring in an outward way the inner spiritual experience of death, burial and resurrection with Christ. The declaration which baptism makes is given in such a striking and vivid fashion that at times in the New Testament the distinction almost disappears between the outward sign and the inner experience signified. As a result language which is strictly applicable to the inner experience is applied to the outward sign. This is seen in Peter's graphic usage where the proclamation of salvation is so clearly made in the ordinance that he writes: 'Baptism . . . now saves you' (1 Peter 3:21). Since some might misinterpret this to teach some quasi-magical power in the water, he immediately adds the important qualification: 'Not the removal of dirt from the body but the pledge of a good conscience towards God.' It is this spiritual reality which is always in view, but such is the potent symbolism of baptism, that Peter moves easily from the sign to the thing signified, from the outward symbol to the inward reality.

The same is true in Paul's treatment of the subject. The spiritual reality in view in Romans 6 is our identification with Christ. This identification was eternally a reality in the saving purpose of God. It was at the heart of Christ's work on the cross when He died in the place of sinners, so that we were with Him representatively at Calvary. It becomes experimentally true for us in our regeneration. The Christian was born 'in Adam' but through the new birth he is 'in Christ'. The man he was in Adam has died and been buried. The new man he is 'in Christ' has been raised to newness of life. Having been united with Christ in His death and burial He is united with Christ in His resurrection. His baptism, with its vivid imagery of burial and rising again, sets forth this truth.

It is the same theme in Colossians 2. In face of the emergence of false teaching at Colosse, Paul insists on the perfection of the work of God in the heart of the believer. There is no need for angelic mediators, for Christ is the perfect Mediator. There is no need for ascetic practices to achieve fulness of life, for in the new creation God has already given them spiritual life. Paul uses the analogy of circumcision. In the Old Testament ordinance the cutting away of the flesh of the organ of procreation symbolized the need for radical spiritual surgery applied to human nature. It was thus an outward sign of regeneration. It is this inner significance of circumcision which is carried forward, for it is a circumcision 'not done by the hands of men' of which Paul speaks. The reality to which the Old Testament prophetically pointed is even fuller. It is not simply the cutting away of one piece of flesh, but the 'putting off of the sinful nature'.

It is in this context that Paul introduces the subject of baptism by way of explaining and illustrating the point he has been making. So he writes that we, who have experienced the circumcision made without hands, the inner renewal of the Holy Spirit, have been 'buried with him in baptism and raised with him'. The new birth has involved a death to sin, and a new birth to righteousness. The old man has been crucified and buried, and the new man raised. It is this spiritual burial and resurrection which are graphically represented in the immersion and rising from the water of the one being baptized.

Since the believer who is baptized has already experienced the miracle of the new birth, it is clear that baptism is not the means by which that new birth is effected. Baptismal regeneration is completely ruled out! Baptism certainly is the instrument by which God proclaims the new birth, but it is not a sacramental channel along which grace flows. Its

administration is closely identified with regeneration, but the
the very fact that it follows rather than precedes it, indicates
that it is not a word spoken to the seeker, but rather to the
one who has found in Christ the answer to his quest. In other
words it is primarily a word of assurance to the Christian that
he has truly become a new man in Christ. It is as if the Lord
were addressing him personally in his baptism: 'You are My
child, born again of My Spirit. You have died to the old life
and risen to the new. Now as your body is buried and raised
from the water, I am declaring to you with assuring power
the reality of what I have done for you.'

A word of challenge

Baptism is, however, not only a word of assurance but one of
challenge. Paul in his letter to the Colossians proceeds to
draw out the implication of being raised to new life. It means
an end to legalism of every kind and an introduction to
Christian liberty. It means also an insistent and continuing
call to daily holiness: 'Since, then, you have been raised with
Christ, set your hearts on things above, where Christ is seated
at the right hand of God. Set your minds on things above,
not on earthly things. For you died and your life is now
hidden with Christ in God' (Col. 3:1-3). This involves a
resolute determination to engage in ruthless self-discipline.
'Put to death, therefore, whatever belongs to your earthly
nature: sexual immorality, impurity, lust, evil desires and
greed, which is idolatry' (3:5). Nor is this holiness to be construed only in negative terms but rather of positive and
practical godliness: 'Therefore, as God's chosen people, holy
and dearly loved, clothe yourselves with compassion, kind-
ness, humility, gentleness and patience' (3:12).

Baptism is thus not only a word to encourage confidence,
but is also a trumpet-call from God to holy living. The assurance which it proclaims is not an excuse for slackness or un-
disciplined living. For a man to make his baptismal profession
of faith a prelude to self-centred living is to face the withering
rebuke of Paul in Romans 6:2, where he rejects with horror
the idea that we may continue to sin in a light-hearted fashion.
To be born again, to profess faith in Christ, to receive the
word declared in baptism — all this is to say farewell to pride,
ungodliness and unrighteousness. It is nothing less than a per-

sonal commitment to a life worthy of the high calling to which God in grace has summoned us.

There is a further note struck in the preaching of the visible word. While baptism is a personal and individual experience, it is never an isolated one. It is not simply a dialogue between God and the one who is baptized, for others are involved. The act of baptism incorporates us into the fellowship of the people of God. 'We were all baptised in one Spirit into one body' (1 Cor. 12:13). Our spiritual rebirth was not only a personal renewal, but involved our membership in the family of the reborn; and it is this introduction to the fellowship of God's elect which is reinforced by baptism. Paul has the same thought as he writes to the Galatians: 'For all of you who were baptised into Christ have been clothed with Christ. There is neither Jew nor Greek, slave nor free, male nor female, for you are all one in Christ Jesus' (Gal. 3:27-28). Baptism is a standing rebuke to apartheid, aloofness and snobbery. Rather it is a warm invitation to enter into the shared life of the church of God.

In all that has been said there is no intention of undervaluing the importance of baptism as an open profession of faith. To the early Christians it was precisely that. In their baptism they not only identified themselves openly with the Christian fellowship, but often virtually signed their own death warrant by such a public commitment. In a similar fashion, in many an Islamic country, baptism has marked the decisive, and often very costly step of open witness. Association with Christians may be tolerated and even a quiet discipleship may be allowed. But baptism is a public and unequivocal avowal which cannot be ignored. The baptized Christian has declared in the most clear-cut terms possible that he has become a disciple of Jesus of Nazareth. Like the Ethiopean eunuch who had received the gospel, he has faced the question: 'Why shouldn't I be baptised?' (Acts 8:37.) Like Saul of Tarsus, he has given heed to the word which Ananias brought to the apostle: 'What are you waiting for? Get up, be baptised and wash your sins away, calling on his name' (Acts 22:16). The physical cost in some countries may not be so real, nor the step viewed in some communities as a form of religious apostasy; but whatever the land and whatever the culture, baptism remains the decisive commitment to whole-hearted discipleship.

Baptism by its very nature is a landmark. It is clearly intended in the New Testament to be a reference point to which the Christian returns in thought again and again. That is why Paul can so clearly use it as his illustration in Romans 6. The passage is not primarily concerned with baptism but with holy living. Yet it seems altogether appropriate for the apostle to recall them to the spiritual landmark standing at the beginning of their Christian life. In face of every specious suggestion that they may lower their spiritual standards, he reminds them firmly of their baptism. In that ordinance God committed them to holiness, and in their submission to baptism they gladly accepted that summons. No matter how long they may live, that memory must still remain as a rallying call from God. When tempted to compromise with the world, or to give way to spiritual sloth, the recollection of their baptism stings them with its rebuke and stirs them afresh to godliness.

Baptism speaks primarily to the person being baptized, but it also speaks to the congregation who are present. In a pioneer situation, where the Christian is the first convert, there may only be one other believer present, namely the missionary who baptizes him. But in fact it is basically the same position as in the more normal situation of a baptism administered in the presence of a worshipping congregation, in that the visible word is addressed to them all whether to the administrator of the ordinance himself, or to the gathered people of God. It comes to them as a word from God. It is a vivid reminder of their own baptism. It is a searching word, as it exposes sinful failure or backsliding, and calls afresh to repentance. But it is also an assuring word, not only to the one being baptized, but to the members of the fellowship. The God who brought each one of them to the birth, and who assured them of their acceptance in their own baptism, is still their God. The word He is speaking to the brother or sister in the water, is being spoken to them as well. It is the abiding word of grace and mercy. The response demanded is also still the same as it was at the beginning — repentance, faith and obedience. Paul really summarizes it in his word to the Colossians: 'So then, just as you received Christ Jesus as Lord, continue to live in him, rooted and built up in him, strengthened in the faith as you were taught, and overflowing with thankfulness' (Col. 2:6-7).

8 Christ our Passover

All our thinking about the Lord's supper must begin with the night when Jesus was betrayed, for it was then that He instituted the supper as a continuing ordinance for His church. To appreciate the wealth of meaning in the Lord's supper we will need to turn to other areas of the New Testament. We will want to study the Lord's discourse in John 6 on eating His flesh and drinking His blood. We will turn to the Acts to see how the early disciples responded to His command as they met together for 'the breaking of the bread'. We will need to examine carefully what the apostle Paul says on the subject in 1 Corinthians 10 and 11. But our starting-point must be the upper room and the account of the institution. Paul in fact starts there, for his explanation of the supper and his insistence on worthy participation are rooted in a full recital of the Lord's words of institution.

To turn to the narrative of the last night in the upper room is, however, to find our thoughts directed beyond that occasion to the Old Testament. After all, the reason for their meeting together was to celebrate the Passover. Jesus had already sent His disciples in advance, not only to find the divinely provided room for the celebration, but also to make ready. His deep concern to share in the Passover with His disciples was expressed in His own words to them: 'I have eagerly desired to eat this Passover with you before I suffer' (Luke 22:15). His words find an echo in Paul's description of the Saviour and in his subsequent call to holy living: 'Christ, our Passover lamb, has been sacrificed. Therefore let us keep the Festival, not with the old yeast, the yeast of malice and wickedness, but with bread without yeast, the bread of sincerity and truth' (1 Cor. 5:7-8).

Nor was the Passover merely a convenient time for instituting the new meal of the people of God. It was in fact the most appropriate occasion, for it was to provide the framework for the new service. While the Passover would give way to the Lord's supper so that the observance of the latter would terminate the yearly festival, it would not be a case of a completely new ordinance abrogating an archaic one, for the new meal emerged out of the old like a flower emerging from the bud. The truths declared by the Passover are not ignored or repudiated, but are in fact filled out with a richer content and a deeper meaning in the Lord's supper. This means that if we are to grasp the significance of the supper we must first study the Old Testament ordinance which throws a flood of light on the essential elements in the ordinance of the New Testament.

At the heart of the Passover was the killing of the lamb, just as in every household the lamb had been killed through the centuries since that first night when, on the eve of their deliverance from Egypt, the Israelites had taken their lambs and sprinkled the blood on the lintel and the doorposts of their homes. But now the Lamb of God has come. He is about to shed His blood as the final sacrifice for sin. He presides over His guests as they meet to recall that first Passover and as He prepares for the final blood-shedding of the next day. The message of what to them was a familiar occasion is filled with a new content as He takes the lessons which the Passover taught and draws from them the implications for the supper He is now instituting. What then were these truths embodied in the Passover?

Recollection

This was the annual festival when every Jewish household looked back with thanksgiving to the great landmark in their history. Whether they met with the pilgrims who thronged Jerusalem, or in some northern Galilean village, or far away in one of the lands of the Jewish dispersion, they all had their thoughts focused on the historic night in Egypt. The very details of the feast recalled not only the deliverance, but the manner of their departure. There were the bitter herbs which recalled the years of harsh captivity and slavery under the Pharaohs. There was the glass of salt water to remind them of the crossing of the Red Sea in the final breach with Egypt.

There were the cups of blood-red wine to press further into their minds the thought of the blood of the Passover lamb which had been the instrument to ensure their deliverance.

So it was essentially a feast of remembrance. They recalled how as a people they had been gripped by the hopeless despair of a bondage which crushed their life. But God had been gracious, and so they recalled with praise His great deliverance. Now Jesus takes up these themes. He had come to save His people from their sins, to set them free from the tyranny of Satan, to deliver them from the bitterness of spiritual bondage, and to set their feet towards the heavenly Canaan. To accomplish all this, He had come to die as the divinely provided Substitute who would avert the judgement hanging over His people and procure their pardon. Thus, just as the Lord gave Israel a meal to be a continuing reminder of the deliverance from Egypt, so He will give the new Israel a meal to recall an even greater deliverance at an infinitely greater cost and with a far more glorious goal in view.

Recital

When the Lord outlined the instructions for the first Passover in Exodus 12 He spoke of the continuing observance when they reached Canaan and of the way they were to respond to the question of their children: 'What does this ceremony mean to you?' They were to reply by way of explanation: 'It is the Passover sacrifice to the Lord, who passed over the houses of the Israelites in Egypt and spared our homes when he struck down the Egyptians' (Exod. 12:26,27). The Jewish oral law, the *Mishnah,* which was in existence by the end of the second century A.D. but had its roots very much earlier, developed this element in the Passover in its instructions for the observance. The son of the family, or the youngest member of the company, was to ask the significance of the feast: 'Why is this night distinguished from all other nights?' Then the father would turn to Deuteronomy 26:5 and expound the history of the exodus. So the Passover was to be the annual recital of the great foundation truths of God's redemption of His people, and was thus a fitting prelude to the recital in the Lord's supper of the greater redemption effected at Calvary.

Rejoicing

There was an obvious difference in the procedure for observ-
ing the first Passover and that which prevailed when Jesus
met with His disciples. The Israelites observed it with their
cloaks tucked into their belts, their sandals on their feet and
their staffs in their hands, all ready for the coming journey.
But as we can see from the way Jesus and His disciples reclined
at the table, the Passover had become a feast of rejoicing. In
subsequent Jewish history it was essentially a joyful festival.
Well beforehand preparations were made. The house was
spring-cleaned and special clothes were prepared for the
occasion. The feast began with a recitation of the *Hallel* or
Praise — Psalms 113-114 — and ended with the second part of
the *Hallel* — Psalms 115-118, the hymn which Jesus and His
disciples sang before they left the upper room to go to the
garden where He was betrayed.

It was fitting therefore that the Lord should use this joyful festival as the context for the new feast of remembrance.
While the actual observance in the upper room was deeply
shadowed, not only by His coming death, but by the disciples'
sad failure, yet at the same time it was anticipating the joy
which lay ahead. Hebrews 12:2 speaks of 'the joy set before
him' which enabled Him to endure the cross. So the Passover
in the upper room, with its joyful recollection of the redemption from Egypt, was the occasion for instituting a meal which
would look forward beyond the darkness of Golgotha to the
glad exultation of the resurrection morning.

Renewing the covenant

Israel was essentially the people of the covenant. In Egypt
they were a demoralized community of slaves, but God
brought them out and constituted them as a nation. But He
did more than give them a sense of national identity. He made
a covenant with them at Sinai in which He pledged Himself
to be their God and summoned them into an intimate relationship with Himself, as His people. He declared to them the
blessings of the covenant and backed His promises with His
own character. At the same time he laid down firmly the
obligations of covenant fellowship and the heavy penalties
which would be meted out if they disobeyed.

Each Passover thus became an annual renewal of the covenant. As they met around the table it was as if God was saying to them: 'You are My people,' and they were replying, 'And You are our God.' A striking illustration of this idea of renewing the covenant is seen in the reign of Hezekiah (2 Chron. 30). After the period of national apostasy from the covenant in the reign of Ahaz, Hezekiah led the people in repentance and in a restoration of the worship of Jehovah. The public declaration of this renewal of the covenant which their unfaithfulness had so sadly breached was the great Passover celebration at the beginning of his reign.

Yet in spite of such periods of spiritual awakening, Israel continued to break the terms of the covenant. It was in a period of such serious national breach that Jeremiah declared the coming glory of the new covenant with its richer promises and greater outpouring of the Spirit. With the coming of the Messiah, and with the shedding of His blood, the new covenant was inaugurated. The upper room was thus the transition moment with a backward look to the covenant made with Israel by God their Redeemer, and a forward look to the new covenant so vividly declared in the Lord's supper.

Reunion

Passover season brought families together. Wherever they were, they would aim if possible to be at home for the Passover. The father of the family would preside as together they recalled the Lord's mercies. So we see Jesus presiding as Head of the family of faith which He has called into being by His gracious ministry. Demonstrating the lesson by His own humble readiness to play the role of the slave in washing their feet, He taught them that they were united as those who were in debt to the mercy of God. They must therefore show their gratitude in willing service rendered to each other. Though He would soon be leaving them He would still preside through His Spirit at their breaking of bread, and because each one of them was united with Him, they would be knit together with each other. That living unity emerging out of the family experience of a Passover meal would be embodied and set forth each time they met at the Lord's table.

With a Gentile background, it is hard to sense the joyful

significance of the Passover for the lineal descendants of the redeemed Israelites. One can, however, detect their sense of wonder and gladness both in the great Passover seasons of the Old Testament and in the evident delight of Jesus in the festival. It is in this glad feast with its thankful remembrance, its proclamation of God's grace, its renewal of the covenant and its cementing of family unity, that we see the truths which would burst into full flower in the Lord's supper.

9 The Lord's supper

Two basic questions confront us as we reflect on the meaning of the Lord's supper. In what sense is Christ present? What is the purpose in view in celebrating the ordinance? To these two questions grievously unbiblical answers have been given. The presence of Christ has been located in the elements so that Christ is alleged to be truly present in bodily fashion under the appearance of bread and wine. The doctrine of what is termed 'the real presence' is the attempt to assert this notion, and behind it is the idea of an essential change in the elements, so that what were substantially bread and wine become after the words of consecration substantially the actual body and blood of Christ. The term used to describe this supposed change is 'transubstantiation'.

Closely allied to the teaching that Christ is really present in the actual elements is the further assertion that the purpose of the supper is to offer a sacrifice to God, both to turn away His wrath which is directed against our sins, and also to be an effective instrument to procure His favourable response to our prayers. The most developed expression of this sacrificial interpretation of the Lord's supper is the Roman Catholic doctrine of the mass, though it is also, with varying modifications, widely accepted in Anglican and in some free church circles.

To deal with these erroneous ideas requires a sustained biblical and historical analysis which would not really be in place in this present book. In any case the reader may see the arguments for and against the Roman Catholic teaching dealt with in a fuller and more detailed fashion in other works on the dogmas of the church of Rome.[1] Suffice it to say that the twin dogmas of transubstantiation and the mass do not

1. See for example H. M. Carson, *Dawn or Twilight?*, I.V.P., 1976.

stand up to the scrutiny either of Scripture or of the history of Christian thought or indeed, in the case of transubstantiation, to that of common sense.

What may profitably be noted here is the manner of their development and also the underlying doctrinal error, for both these issues are recurring factors in many other areas. In the matter of the development of the dogmas one can see a clear illustration of what happens when the church begins to conform her life and teaching to the culture and thought patterns of the contemporary world. In the fourth century such a tragic conformity was well under way. The unexpected change of fortunes when formerly persecuted churches became the favoured communities of the Roman empire led to a paganizing of the churches as nominal adherents flooded into the now respectable institution. Pagan ideas of sacrifices offered by priests with quasi-magical powers in order to propitiate the deity and to win his favour, began to spread into the churches. It took centuries until the dogma of transubstantiation finally emerged in 1215 A.D. and the dogma of the mass was formulated at the Council of Trent, but long before their formulation the seeds of error sown centuries before had taken deep root.

Behind the historical development, however, there is a more fundamental error. It is the one noted earlier in the chapter on baptism. It is the adoption of the wrong starting-point, so that the primary point of reference is man rather than God. It begins with man and his consciously realized needs, continues with man in his efforts to find God and ends by making the grace of God little more than a helping hand. Instead of the biblical view of grace as the free favour of the Almighty extended to helpless, ignorant and undeserving sinners, grace is seen as a co-operative enterprise in which God is matching the efforts man has already made.

When all this is applied to the Lord's supper it turns the ordinance back to front. Instead of asking what God says and does, it begins with man's words and actions. Such thinking inevitably moves in the direction of the sacrifice of the mass. Liberal Roman Catholics and Anglo-Catholics try to refine the crudities of the traditional presentation of eucharistic sacrifice. They speak of the worshipping congregation identifying themselves with 'the eternal self-offering of Christ' — a concept which is absent from the New Testament. They are still following the same unbiblical idea which envisages man presenting a sacrifice to God. It appears in Bright's communion hymn:

> We here present, we here spread forth to Thee
> That only offering perfect in Thine eyes
> The one true, pure, immortal sacrifice.

If, on the other hand, we view the Lord's supper as 'the visible word' proclaimed by a gracious God to a listening and obedient people we move into a completely different realm of thought. The service ceases to be primarily our approach to God and is seen, as it truly is, as God's declaration to us. It declares that pardon is offered and spiritual strength is given because Christ's body has been offered once and for all, and His blood has been shed. His body is not being continually broken nor His blood endlessly shed. The sacrifice was offered once and for all and was accepted by God. There is nothing to add. Any attempt to present again to God the sacrifice of Calvary would be an insult alike to the Son, for it would cast doubts on the perfection of His work, and to the Father, for it would query the veracity of His acceptance of Christ's finished work. Each Lord's supper declares to us, 'Redemption is finished, the price has been paid.' What is required is not some attempt to re-enact Calvary but humble gratitude and responsive faith.

This brings us back to our basic questions. In what sense is Christ present and what is the purpose in view as we celebrate the Lord's supper? Our reply to the first question is that Christ is present, not in any material or localized sense, but in a dynamic way as He accomplishes His promises. His word of grace is vividly declared in the giving and receiving, in the eating and drinking. But He not only speaks His word but accompanies that word with His own presence and power. Nor does he accompany it only to the threshold of our thinking, for He steps across the threshold to write His promises in our hearts. So we may say that His presence is to be found not only in the promises declared in the supper, but also in the hearts of His believing people. We reject the Roman Catholic notion of 'the real presence', but we do not preach by contrast 'a real absence'! We believe that Christ is truly present for He is the One who presides at the table and who stirs His people by the power of His Spirit to throw open the door of their hearts for His gracious coming. So we delight to sing Spurgeon's communion hymn:

> Amidst us our Beloved stands,
> And bids us view His pierced hands;
> Points to His wounded feet and side,
> Blest emblems of the Crucified.

To the further question: 'What is the purpose of the supper?' the answer has been given that the aim is to plead with God. Our reply to that erroneous notion is the observation that it is not God who needs to be reminded of Calvary, but we ourselves. We do not need to display the cross before God to elicit His response to our needs. Rather He displays Christ before us to elicit from us the response of repentance, faith, obedience and love. Our aim is not to offer a sacrifice to move God to be favourable to us, but to bow before Him in expectant faith as He declares afresh to us the glory of the sacrifice of Christ already offered. We come just as we do when the Word is preached, to hear what God has to say to us, in order that we might give ourselves to Him in renewed submission.

The message of grace

What then does God say to us as we meet at His table? What message do the bread and wine thrust into our faces and indeed into our mouths? It is in the first place the proclamation of God's grace, that He is the God who delights to give. He is not like the tight-fisted employer who carefully apportions payment for the amount of work performed by the employee. He is rather the generous benefactor whose liberality overflows, not only to the needy, but to those who have slighted his previous offers, slandered his character and ignored his approaches. God is the great Giver whose generosity to the totally undeserving is summed up in Paul's description of Christ as God's 'indescribable gift' (2 Cor. 9:15). One of the basic texts of Scripture is the Lord's own statement: 'God so loved the world that he gave his one and only Son' (John 3:16). Paul draws out the full implications of this fundamental gift as he reflects on the overwhelming goodness of God: 'He who did not spare his own Son, but gave him up for us all — how will he not also, along with him, graciously give us all things?' (Rom. 8:32.)

The Lord's supper displays this biblical pattern with its stress on what God has done, what God provides and what God promises. The 'movement' of the supper is from God to us, and then from us to God. It is primarily a declaration of God's gracious initiative and then, as a consequence, of the response required. The narrative of the institution in the upper room brings this home forcibly. There is no prompting by the disciples, nor any initial approach on their part. Jesus takes the initiative as He institutes the supper, and He Himself is completely in control. He takes the bread and the cup; He gives them to the disciples; He adds the words of explanation; He bids them eat and drink. The food freely given by the Lord to His guests is a visual representation of the pattern of God's dealing with His people — He is the great Donor, the Giver of 'every good and perfect gift' (James 1:17).

God has already given, but He continues to give and will still give. His giving has past, present and future dimensions. He gave His Son to die for our sins and to be raised for our justification. Daily He gives us His Holy Spirit and with Him come all the graces and gifts needed for life. He has pledged Himself to continue to give to us in the future, so that we can sing with the psalmist: 'Surely goodness and love will follow me all the days of my life' (Ps. 23:6).

The Lord's supper proclaims the giving God in all the dimensions of His generous activity. In its emphasis on the completion of the work of redemption it turns our minds back to the cross, and to God's gift of His Son so freely given for the salvation of sinners. Yet at the same time it reminds us of His continuing liberality. 'Take and eat . . . drink this' — the invitation repeated at every communion is a constant reminder that the God who gave still delights to give. 'His compassions never fail. They are new every morning' (Lam. 3:22-23). Each new day brings fresh temptations, new problems, the continuing assaults of Satan, the unremitting pressure of the world. But each new day the faithful God is with us to give us pardon and cleansing, to give us afresh His Holy Spirit, to assure us of His presence. Each Lord's supper is His ringing word of reassurance. '"Never will I leave you; never will I forsake you." So we say with confidence, "The Lord is my helper; I will not be afraid. What can man do to me?"' (Heb. 13:5.)

The future dimension is also present in the continuing observance of the Lord's supper, for it is to be celebrated regularly 'until He comes'. It points forward to the second coming, not as a possible outcome of historical trends but as the certain consummation of the plan of God. In declaring the coming of the Lord, the supper pledges to us the continuance to the end of God's faithfulness. He will not falter in the outworking of His purposes. He will not run short of resources to accomplish His will. There will never be a situation beyond His ability to control. There will never be a time when His people will look in vain for forgiveness. There will be no stain in the future too deep for the cleansing power of Christ's blood. There will be no burden too heavy for Him to bear.

At the Lord's table Christ invites us to receive His gifts of bread and wine. In the very act of giving these symbols of nourishment for our bodies and slaking of our thirst, He is displaying His readiness to give. In His ministry to us He is the spokesman for His Father, the Creator who gave us life itself and all things richly to enjoy, the Sustainer who daily gives us health and strength, and the Redeemer who furnishes us with every spiritual blessing. This united testimony of the Father and the Son is brought home to us by the Holy Spirit who takes the gracious message of the visible word and applies it to eyes and hands and tongue and taste, and even more powerfully to mind and heart and will.

The proclamation of the cross

The focus of the Lord's supper is the death of Christ. As God proclaims in the bread and wine His free gift of a Saviour, it is the crucified Saviour to whom we are directed. Indeed not only does God proclaim the death of Christ to us but we echo His declaration as we proclaim that death to one another. Admittedly our mutual testimony is but a faint echo of the trumpet-call of heaven, but none the less it is the same message. Throughout the supper, whether in the words of institution with their gracious invitation to receive the gifts, or in our own reception of these gifts, God is displaying to us and we are sharing together in the great fundamental truth of the gospel that Christ died for our sins.

This centrality of the cross in the message of the supper tallies with the emphasis throughout the New Testament, where the theme of Christ crucified is at the heart of the revelation given in the apostolic testimony. It is seen, for example, in the very structure of the Gospels. Normal biographies spend time on the background of their subject and the achievements of his life. But the Gospels give what might seem, to the uninstructed outsider, to be an undue amount of space to the events of the final week, and even more to the final hours of Jesus' life. Clearly their purpose in writing was to highlight the supreme importance of Calvary.

The same is true in the preaching. When Paul recalled to the Corinthians his initial visit to them and the preaching they heard he stressed its essential content: 'I resolved to know nothing while I was with you except Jesus Christ and him crucified' (1 Cor. 2:2). He was fully aware with his Jewish upbringing and his rabbinic training that this message was an affront to the Jews, as it still is to all who pin their hopes on their own efforts to win favour with God. So, too, with his Greek education he knew the scornful contempt with which the intellectuals dismissed his gospel as foolishness. But he was unmoved by it all and asserted with confidence: 'We preach Christ crucified: a stumbling block to Jews and foolishness to Gentiles, but to those whom God has called, both Jews and Greeks, Christ the power of God and the wisdom of God' (1 Cor. 1:23-24).

The theme of Christ crucified, preached by ministers of the gospel and set forth vividly at the Lord's table, remains the theme of the glorified saints in heaven. The vision of John on the island of Patmos is one in which God draws aside the veil and gives us a glimpse of the surpassing wonder of heaven. The throng of people drawn from every tribe and nation and tongue continues the theme which has dominated the life of the church down the centuries. The Lord's supper has now given way to the marriage supper of the Lamb, but the theme of praise remains the same. So we hear those who rejoiced on earth to sing the praise of a crucified Saviour joining now in the exultant strains of the chorus of the redeemed: 'To him who loves us and has freed us from our sins by his blood, and has made us to be a kingdom and priests to serve his God and Father — to him be glory and power for ever! Amen!' (Rev. 1:5-6.) Whether then it is the audible word preached from the pulpit, or the visible word declared at the Lord's table, the heart of the message remains the same, for it is Christ crucified.

That declaration of His death begins with the reason for His crucifixion. There were clearly a number of factors in the situation which led to the cross. There was the bitter hostility of the ecclesiastics, who plotted His death and were prepared to stoop to any method, even perjury, to accomplish their end. There was the cowardice of Pilate, who should have administered the law with the traditional impartiality of a Roman judge. There were the humbler human agents involved — the soldiers who stripped Him and scourged Him, mocked Him and finally nailed Him to the tree. But beyond all these factors there was a hidden one of supreme importance. After all, Jesus could have escaped their hands, and as He Himself said in Gethsemane, could have summoned legions of angels to help Him. But He did neither for He recognized and gladly accepted the ultimate reason for His death. That reason is well summed up by Isaiah: 'It was the Lord's will to crush him and cause him to suffer' (Isa. 53:10). So it is that every time we are reminded at the Lord's table that the body of Christ was given for us and His blood was shed for us, we are being pointed to the One who ultimately gave Him to the cross. Abraham had been ready to sacrifice Isaac but God spared the lad and set him free. But, says Paul, 'He . . . did not spare his own Son, but gave him up for us all' (Rom. 8:32).

There is a further truth about the death of Christ declared to us in the supper: it is the utter finality of it. His death, says Scripture again and again, was 'once for all' and the sacrifice was complete, never to be repeated. When Jesus cried out on the cross, 'It is finished,' it was not the weakening cry of a dying man, but the confident shout of a conqueror whose work was complete. To quote the superb words of Thomas Cranmer's communion service, 'He made there by his one oblation of himself once offered, a full perfect and sufficient sacrifice for the sins of the whole world.'

In the upper room there was a marked break between the giving of the bread and the wine. It was after supper that He took the cup. The interval dramatizes the separation of the body and blood which comes in death. It is stressing the finality of His offering. It can pass without our noticing but it is worthy of observation that in our communion service we preserve, even if in an attenuated form, this disjunction of bread and wine. There is the giving of thanks for the bread and its distribution. Then afterwards comes the giving of the cup. Displayed in that very order is the sundering of His body and blood by death.

There is more to the rich declaration of His death in the supper. It is bread which is broken and wine poured out which are the messages to us. He did not die in the quiet of His home surrounded by His friends. He was brutally done to death on a Roman scaffold. Blood in the veins speaks of life, but blood shed speaks of death. And it is the death which is set forth. Nor is it only in terms of the violence employed; it speaks of His death as that of a sacrificial victim who died in His people's place.

The broken bread declares to us His broken body. It is evident, however, from the prayers offered at the Lord's table that Christians find it more difficult to grasp the significance of the breaking of His body. The shedding of His blood they can understand, for the Passover lamb is a vivid word of explanation. But what is the truth presented by the breach of His body? In reply, we ask the purpose which His body served as far as His life and ministry were concerned. It was in the first place the vehicle of His obedience. When He became incarnate in the womb of Mary it was the actual moment of self-humbling described so vividly by Paul as 'taking the very nature of a servant' (Phil. 2:7). Furthermore it was the instrument of His ministry. His feet carried Him on errands of mercy. His eyes saw the need of men and women. His hands reached out to touch the leper and to bless the children, and were finally stretched out on the cross. So His body speaks of His total obedience to the Father's will and when that body was broken on the tree it was the final stage in that submission. 'He became obedient to death — even death on a cross!' (Phil. 2:8.)

But the bread is given to those who come in penitence. The word is personal: 'The body of Christ was broken for you.' God confronts us with our own unrighteousness. We have utterly failed to reach the standard of righteousness which the law imposes. The cry of the heart is for a righteousness which will satisfy the demands of a holy God. Here, says the Father, is a perfect righteousness. It was wrought out in the actual bodily life of the incarnate One, and is set to the account of those who, having despaired of their own goodness, have turned to Christ and found in Him a righteousness adequate to face the scrutiny of the Day of Judgement.

If the broken bread speaks of His broken body and so of His active obedience, then the cup speaks of His shed blood and so of His willing acceptance of the penalty of our disobedience. He was not only the unique law-keeper, he was also the One who graciously accepted the guilt of the law-breakers. He obeyed God's law on behalf of His unrighteous people, and He suffered the consequences of their breach of that law by shedding His precious blood. Each time the broken bread is on the table and in our hands and mouths, it reminds us of His broken body. It is preaching to us afresh the glory of His righteousness, perfected as it was in His death, which has been set to our account.

If the emphasis on the gift of His body is on the perfect righteousness accomplished on our behalf, then the shedding of His blood stresses the penalty which was paid, the guilt which was borne, and the consequent cleansing which is ours by faith in that shed blood. The broken body speaks of His complete obedience and His shed blood underlines the finality of His sacrifice, and the never-to-be-repeated sacrifice which has met the full demands of the outraged justice of God. In both cases there is a strongly personal emphasis: 'This is my body for you; . . . this is my blood which is shed for you.' As His words are spoken, and as the bread and the cup are placed in our hands, the Lord is reminding us that His death was not a detached judicial event, but had in view the particular people whom He had come to redeem.

The covenant meal

Dig deeply into the Scriptures in order to discover the basic doctrines, and inevitably one comes to the word 'covenant'. Here is the key to the understanding of the biblical revelation. The doctrinal phrase, 'the covenant of grace', is not simply one in the list of biblical truths; rather it expresses the very essence of the religion of Scripture. The Bible, in short, is the book of the covenant, and the God who is revealed there is the One who saves sinful men and women and brings them into a covenant relationship with Himself.

The essential elements in any covenant are the people involved, the promises made and the conditions laid down and accepted. In the marriage covenant, for example, two people enter into a solemn union, with promises made and responsibilities undertaken. There is, however, a fundamental difference between any human covenant and the one which God makes with His people. In the former the contracting parties each make their contribution, whereas in the covenant between God and men, He alone is the giver. It is essentially a gracious covenant in which God takes the initiative, makes the promises and lays down the conditions.

When the Jewish translators in Alexandria were rendering the Old Testament into Greek, they faced a choice of words to translate the Hebrew word *berith*. There were two possibilities — *suntheke* and *diatheke*. The former word, however, implied a contract between two contributing parties, and as a result was not suitable to convey the stress in the word *berith*, on the sovereign grace of God. The word *diatheke* on the other hand had as its root meaning a sovereign disposal of one's property. As such it was the obvious word to use and so it not only appears in the Septuagint version of the Old Testament, but is used by the writers of the Greek New Testament to continue the same emphasis on the sovereign grace of God.

By the time the New Testament was being written the word *diatheke* had come to be employed in current Greek usage for a will. In view of the English phrase 'the last will and testament' it is not surprising that the translators of the Authorized Version rendered the term *diatheke* by 'testament', and as a result the two volumes of Scripture became known as the Old Testament and the New Testament. In Hebrews 9 the word is used specifically in the sense of will or testament, and is correctly so translated. But elsewhere the main idea in view is the sovereign bestowal of gifts, together with the conditions imposed on the recipients, and a more correct translation would therefore be 'covenant'. Long usage has so embedded the terms Old and New Testaments in our language and thinking that it is unlikely that we will cease to use them.

It is, however, important that we should appreciate that the true meaning of the word is 'covenant'.

The covenant of grace is thus a relationship between God and men in which He condescends to be their God and to make them His people. He is the almighty Creator, yet He stoops to His creatures and pledges Himself to be their God. He is the Holy One who yet in grace reaches down to guilty rebels and not only pardons them but establishes such an intimate relationship that they can call Him Father and lay claim to the fulfilment of His promises. Throughout, God is the Sovereign who decides those whom He will summon, the promises He will make to them and the conditions of obedience which He will impose.

There is a development in the way God revealed Himself as the God of the covenant. He made Himself known with increasing clarity in the various covenants of the Old Testament until He gave His final disclosure in the new covenant of our Lord Jesus Christ. The unfolding of this developing revelation is well summarized in the majestic opening of the Epistle to the Hebrews: 'In the past God spoke to our forefathers through the prophets at many times and in various ways, but in these last days he has spoken to us by his Son.' The dawning light of truth has reached its final climax in the full midday splendour of the revelation of Christ.

The first formulation of the covenant comes with the call of Abraham. Here in Genesis 17 we see this covenant rooted in the electing grace of God who has taken the initiative in calling him and pledges Himself to be Abraham's God. He promises blessing to him and through his offspring to the nations of the earth. He gives him an outward seal of the covenant in the rite of circumcision and requires the answering response of faith and obedience.

The covenant on Sinai is often misunderstood as a covenant of works — that is not surprising since the Israelites made that tragic blunder themselves in their false ideas of winning God's favour by their own religious efforts. In fact it was essentially a covenant of grace or, to be more precise, a further unfolding of that covenant. Thus in Exodus 19:4 it is based on the redemption from Egypt. The law was not given as a way of earning salvation — this was the disastrous error which perverted the meaning of the covenant. The law rather was God's way of deepening an awareness of sin, and so of their total dependence on His pardoning grace and continuing mercy. The law was not intended to be an instrument for winning God's approval, but rather a pointer to the grateful obedience of those who in the covenant had already known the grace of God.

A further important element in the covenant was the place of sacrifice. In the blood-shedding there was a significant manipulation of the blood. It was not only applied to the altar where the victim was offered, but sprinkled on the worshippers. The symbolism clearly speaks of an objective atonement effected by the death of the substitutionary victim, and the application to the penitent believer of the fruits of that atonement. The covenant was thus rooted in the grace of God, promised mercy to those who shared in it and imposed obedience as a thankful response.

It was the continuing failure of Israel to keep the terms of the covenant which led to the recurring judgements of God. Again and again God dealt severely with them because they had flouted the covenant by their rebellion. These judgements reached their grim climax in the exile when the nation was uprooted from the promised land and removed to Babylon. Yet even at that point, when Jeremiah was thundering God's warnings, the persistent grace of God was evident as the prophet spoke of a new covenant. It would continue the pattern of grace embodied in the old covenant but would bring a wealth of blessings which would eclipse all that had gone before.

Jeremiah declared the terms of this new covenant which God would make with His people in the day of the coming of the Messiah: '"The time is coming," declares the Lord, "when I will make a new covenant with the house of Israel and with the house of Judah. It will not be like the covenant I made with their forefathers when I took them by the hand to lead them out of Egypt, because they broke my covenant, though I was a husband to them," declares the Lord. "This is the covenant that I will make with the house of Israel after that time," declares the Lord. "I will put my law in their minds and write it on their hearts. I will be their God, and they will be my people. No longer will a man teach his neighbour, or a man his brother, saying, 'Know the Lord,' because they will all know me, from the least of them to the greatest," declares the Lord. "For I will forgive their wickedness and will remember their sins no more."' (Jer. 31:31-34.)

This promise of the forgiveness of sins is a reminder that the new covenant, like the old, is based on the work of atonement. The blood shed through the slaying of the sacrifice was not only the ground of the covenant at Sinai; it was prophetic of the richer blood-shedding of the final sacrifice for sin which would be necessary if the blessings of the new covenant were to be procured. The Messiah would bring to His people the blessings of the new covenant, but He would also pay the price of those blessings by His own atoning death.

It is with this total background of the old covenant that one can appreciate the meaning of the Lord's words in the upper room: 'This cup is the new covenant in my blood.' The cup, which speaks so vividly of the shed blood of the Lamb of God as the ground of our pardon and acceptance, speaks also of the blessings of the covenant into which forgiven sinners are initiated. Rebels though they were, they are now in intimate relationship with God.

The Lord's supper is thus the covenant meal of the people of God. Each time we meet we are summoned by the grace of God. In His ordinance He declares His grace to us, and displays the cost of our redemption. He reaffirms also the blessings of the covenant. This God is our God and we are His people. He has not only given us the promises of the covenant but He backs those promises with His own character. He binds Himself to fulfil every promise He has made. Amazing though it is, we, who are never anything but sinners saved by the grace of God, may yet come, not only with confidence but even with boldness, to lay claim to the blessings which He has pledged Himself to give.

The covenant meal not only displays in visible symbol the blessings of membership but also reminds us that the people of the covenant must walk worthily of their calling. Yet it is not some legalistic reaction which is demanded, for such a dutiful attitude, with its undertones of merit, has no place in the covenant of grace. Rather it is the glad response of those who are so overwhelmed by the grace of God that their supreme desire is to show their thanksgiving in their obedience to their gracious covenant-keeping God.

10　The Lord's guests

The Word of God demands a response, whether it is preached from the pulpit or displayed at the table. Whether it is the audible or the visible word, God insistently requires the reply of repentance, faith and obedience. As we turn to a consideration of the response of the worshipper at the Lord's supper we must always keep it firmly in the context of the grace of God. The supper, as we have seen, emphasizes the initiative of God, who in grace has given His Son and with Him gives us the blessings of the covenant sealed in the blood of Christ. Our response to the Word is never the contribution which we make to the saving work of God going on in our hearts. Always it is a response prompted by grace and, indeed, made possible by the renewing grace of God within us.

Remembrance

We have already seen that the Lord's supper is not our way of reminding God of Calvary, but God's way of reminding us. God, having planned the atoning death of His Son and having shown His acceptance of that sacrifice by raising and exalting the Saviour, needs no stimulus to stir His memory. He delights in what Christ has done, and by the continuing work of His Spirit declares it to men. It is rather we who need to be stirred. Nor is this stirring needful only at the beginning of the Christian life when the Holy Spirit awakens us from the sleep of sin, convicts us and leads us to the Saviour. Because of our indwelling sin and because of the deadening influence of the world, and the subtle side-tracking suggestions of Satan, we easily become sluggish in our appreciation of Calvary. We need our memories jogged that our hearts may be stirred and our wills moved afresh to obedience. The Lord's supper is God's reminder to a drowsy Christian, bidding him rouse himself afresh to the wonder of the grace of God revealed in the cross of Christ.

The Lord's supper is not, however, simply God's reminder to us to which we respond by a passive acknowledgement of the death of Christ. When the Lord says to His disciples, 'Do this in remembrance of me', He is asking for an active response. We are called on to concentrate with all our powers on the reminder that God is giving us, in order that we may recall it clearly. There are, after all, some things which come unbidden to our minds. The recollection of an old sorrow or a past failure suddenly emerges in our consciousness without any prompting on our part. But there are many matters such as appointments which we have made, or important discussions which we have had, which we have to make an effort to recall. So our remembrance of the Lord at His table is to be quite deliberate. We are to set our minds upon the visible word which God is declaring to us, so that we may recall the dying love of Christ.

In an act of remembrance we endeavour to define with as much precision as possible the issue we are recalling to mind. This act of mental definition involves holding the past before our mind's eye so that its details are vividly before us. As a consequence we seem to enter into the past event. Indeed we speak of living again the experience of years back. This is particularly evident in the case of old people who may be recalling something which happened to them fifty years ago. They see it all happening; they hear the people speaking; and in fact they feel that they are back in the situation. In the same way we remember the death of Christ. We bring the details of Calvary before our minds. We hear His cry of desolation and His shout of triumph. We see Him bow His head and yield up His spirit to His Father. As a result, it is not like a mere historical event which we recall by an effort of the mind. Because God is actively at work reminding us of the cross, our remembrance becomes an active recall in which we feel ourselves to be as deeply involved as the disciples who saw Him die, or the thief who found pardon and an open door to paradise.

To remember the Lord's death is to be deeply moved by what we recall. We cannot call to mind the cross of Christ without being stirred to reverent wonder. To think that it was the Lord of glory who stood alone in the Roman barrack-room as the object of the crude jokes of the soldiers; that it was the Son of God who was nailed to the tree and made a public spectacle; that it was the Holy One who 'was made sin' and cried out in the agony of a man under judgement — all this when recalled to mind moves us to awe and wonder.

It also stirs us to praise and thanksgiving. It is no wonder that the feast of remembrance was called by the first believers 'the eucharist'. The word simply means 'thanksgiving', and the supper was to them in a special way 'the thanksgiving'. It was the service in which the praise and thanks of their hearts could find its focus and its glad expression. The term 'eucharist' has sadly been tarnished by the foreign notions of sacrifice which Rome has associated with it. But its early usage, without the later accretions, is a testimony to the attitude of thanksgiving which characterized the first-century Christians. To remember the Lord was to be moved to the depths by His condescending grace. It was to be stimulated to praise and thanksgiving. That moving and stimulating experience is still a reality to us as we meet at the table to remember Him; and thanksgiving is still the joyful response of adoring hearts.

Participation

The emphasis in the upper room was on the reception of the gifts of bread and wine. The disciples were not sharing in the responsibility of the host; they were in the role of guests. They were not contributors but recipients. This did not mean, nor does it mean, a mere acquiescence, but rather the active participation of faith. One of the homilies of the Anglican Reformers puts it well: 'Every one of us must be guests and not gazers, eaters and not lookers, feeding ourselves and not hiring others to feed us.'[1]

A meal, after all, is not like a cookery demonstration which is essentially for display purposes — though even there we expect someone to sample the results! The object of a meal is simply to feed the guests and to do so with the added enjoyment of appetizing food. The food is taken and assimilated and it becomes part of us, nourishing and strengthening

1. Homily 15.

our bodies. So the Lord's supper is not like the traditional Roman mass, with communion an optional extra. It is essentially a meal in which we participate. So Paul asks, 'Is not the cup of thanksgiving for which we give thanks a participation in the blood of Christ? And is not the bread that we break a participation in the body of Christ?' (1 Cor. 10:16.) The blessings which are declared are for us to make our own. The issue then is — how do we participate spiritually? We do not need any instruction as to eating bread and drinking wine. We do, however, need clear teaching from Scripture if we are to understand how to receive the benefits procured for us by the Saviour.

The Lord's discourse recorded in John 6, while not primarily expounding the Lord's supper, is basic to our understanding. It produced a twofold effect. There was deep perplexity as to its meaning and, with some at least, an indignant reaction which led to the defection of many who had been following among His disciples. Certainly at first reading the words are startling, if not shocking, as Jesus speaks of eating His flesh and drinking His blood and when He insists, 'My flesh is real food and my blood is real drink. Whoever eats my flesh and drinks my blood remains in me, and I in him' (John 6:55-56).

It is clear that the Lord's words must not be interpreted in a baldly literalistic way. It was just such a crude misunderstanding which lay behind the indignant question of the objectors: 'How can this man give us his flesh to eat?' Yet Jesus ruled out any such misinterpretation when he insisted that a merely physical eating and drinking were not in view: 'The Spirit gives life; the flesh counts for nothing. The words I have spoken to you are spirit and they are life.'

The words are thus to be understood in a spiritual sense. We are to feed upon Him by faith with thanksgiving. We are to lay hold of Him by faith in such a way that we will be able to echo Paul's words: 'I no longer live, but Christ lives in me' (Gal. 2:20). Why then, we might ask, did he use such cryptic language? The answer is that, both for Him and for those who heard Him, their common background was a knowledge of the Old Testament. As so often in the Gospels and indeed in the New Testament generally, the puzzling phraseology and enigmatic allusions emerge into clarity when the Old

Testament key is used to unlock the meaning.

The background of the Lord's words here is the peace offerings which formed an integral part of the sacrificial system. The distinctive feature of the peace offering was that, after the animal had been killed and the blood poured out, the worshipper ate the flesh of the sacrificial victim. It was a fellowship meal in which the worshipper was meeting with Jehovah. A shared meal was a mark of friendship and the enjoyment of the meat of the victim was at the same time a renewed experience of friendship with the Lord.

But the very title 'peace offering' implied that before the meal there had been discord. The enjoyment of fellowship was possible because peace had been established where formerly there was a breach. There were therefore two aspects in view in the offering — the ending of hostility and the renewal of friendship. To use two more technical terms, there was first propitiation, and then communion. The substituted victim was presented in place of the sinner and on the basis of the acceptance by Jehovah of the sacrifice there was a welcome for the worshipper into the intimacy of fellowship with his Lord. For an Israelite the most obvious way of recognizing reconciliation with an estranged neighbour was to have a meal with him. It was most appropriate then that, having been reconciled to God, they should meet in the fellowship of a shared meal.

The peace offering, then, is the key to understanding Jesus' words. He is the One whose shed blood is the propitiation on the basis of which God receives into fellowship guilty sinners. But He is also the One through whom we may enjoy communion with God. He not only died to remove our guilt; He lives to draw us into communion with Himself, and so to bring us into a deep fellowship with His Father who is now also our Father. When He speaks therefore of eating His flesh and drinking His blood He is speaking of our sharing in all that He has done for us.

Turning in more detail to the two sides of this participation, we look first at the word about 'eating His flesh'. Earlier we saw that it was in His body that the Lord Jesus perfected the life of righteousness. The broken bread in the supper speaks of the body broken on the cross and declares the completeness of His obedience. It is that perfect righteousness of

Christ which God graciously imputes to the sinner when He freely justifies him for Christ's sake. Now we cannot go on being justified for it is the once-for-all verdict of the divine Judge. Christ's righteousness having been set to our account, we are accepted and nothing can alter that final judicial act. In what sense then do we eat His flesh? Surely in the sense that we remember again and again the perfect obedience of Christ our righteousness, and each time we take the bread in the supper we are returning to the foundation of our Christian life. We reflect afresh on our justification, and rejoice that for Christ's sake we have been accepted as righteous. We enter afresh by faith into the blessings which flow from the never-to-be-repeated declaration of our justifying God.

To be justified is not to be ushered into a state of sinless perfection. Scripture and experience both give the lie to such a notion. In Luther's phrase each one of us is *simul iustus ac peccator,* at one and the same time justified and a sinner. When we sin we give an opportunity to Satan who is well named in Scripture 'the accuser'. In face of his accusation, and particularly in a situation of serious failure, it is sadly possible for us to waver in our assurance and even to doubt our justification. The anguished question springs insistently to our troubled minds: 'Can I be a Christian at all and behave as I have done?' The answer to such self-accusation, reinforced as it is by Satan's condemning voice, is to go back to the basis of our acceptance. It was not because of some inner change in us but because of the perfect work of Christ that we were justified. So we turn back to His perfect righteousness and recognize anew the unassailable grounds of our acceptance. It is to this place of reassurance that the Lord's supper directs us. The broken bread speaks to the troubled heart about the body of the obedient Saviour. I eat the bread in grateful acknowledgement that His obedience is mine. I renew my confidence as by faith I receive afresh the assurance of God Himself that, clothed in the righteousness of Christ, I am, and always will be, complete.

The mention of drinking His blood was the breaking-point for the Jews. The Scriptures forbade the eating of flesh from which the blood had not been drained, and with their crude literalism they thought Jesus was urging precisely that. Yet such an idea was far from His thoughts. After all He accepted the same Scriptures as they did, and endorsed them down to the last detail. He could not possibly be speaking of drinking blood in such a gross fashion. What then did He mean by this puzzling saying?

Again we go to the Old Testament, this time for an illustration of the kind of language He was using. It is found in the incident recorded in 2 Samuel 23, when David was in hiding in the cave of Adullam. He was thirsty, and in a moment of nostalgia recalled many a drink of cold water in his native village. Hence his expressed wish: 'Oh, that someone would get me a drink of water from the well near the gate of Bethlehem!' His wish was as good as a command to his 'mighty men' who broke through the garrison of the Philistines to fetch him the water he had so longed for. David was overwhelmed. How could he drink it since these men had put their lives at risk in going to fetch it? He puts his scruples in vivid language as he pours out the water as an offering to the Lord, and asks, 'Is it not the blood of men who went at the risk of their lives?' (2 Sam. 23:17.) To drink the water would be to enjoy a benefit obtained by hazarding men's lives. For us, however, the benefits of salvation where not obtained by a risk to the life of Jesus, but by His actual death. The cup we take in the Lord's supper speaks even more powerfully to us than the vessel of water spoke to David. We might well adapt his words: 'Is it not the blood of Christ who went at the cost of his life?' When we hear His words: 'This is my blood which is shed for you,' our minds turn to His death. When we hear the further words: 'Drink it in remembrance of me,' our thoughts move to the benefits we receive – continuing forgiveness, the love of God shed abroad in our hearts, access to God, the gift of the Spirit and much else besides! So faith urges us – let us take from His gracious hands all that He has purchased by the shedding of His blood. The hymn of Bernard of Clairvaux might well express our desire for a deepening enjoyment of the fulness of life which is in Christ:

> We taste Thee, O Thou living bread,
> And long to feast upon Thee still;
> We drink of Thee, the fountain-head,
> And thirst our souls from Thee to fill.

Communion

The Lord's supper is not only a personal participation in the blessings procured by the death of Christ; it is a shared participation. When a congregation gathers at the Lord's table, it is not a case of an assortment of individuals, each one receiving by personal faith the blessings of God. It is a shared experience. It is a communion service, in that we who share a common experience of the new birth, we who have been baptized into the body of Christ, share together in the gifts of the Lord. So Paul puts his questions in 1 Corinthians 10:16: 'Is not the cup . . . a participation in the blood of Christ? Is not the bread . . . a participation in the body of Christ?' But immediately he adds the firm reminder that this participation must not be construed in any individualistic fashion: 'Because there is one loaf, we, who are many, are one body, for we all partake of the one loaf.'

The unity of Christians is not seen in the New Testament as a goal to be reached, but as an already existing reality to be maintained. The disciples were taught to pray in a corporate way: 'Our Father'. Paul urges an awareness of how completely we belong together as he calls us to 'rejoice with those who rejoice; mourn with those who mourn' (Rom. 12:15). So, too, he insists, in his treatment of the gifts of the Spirit, that their use must spring from an awareness of our interdependence within the body of Christ, and must be controlled by our concern to build up one another.

In a shared meal we enjoy the social contact with others. When it is a family gathering after a time when some members have been absent, the meal is not just a routine satisfaction of our hunger, but is a time of enjoyable reunion. The Lord's supper is such a reunion. The family of God in the local congregation meets together at the table. During the week we are out of touch with each other. Some are in their place of work, a lone Christian voice perhaps in a babel of ungodliness. Others have been facing problems or sickness. Still others may have had some particular blessing. But all of us come together on the Lord's Day and at the Lord's table we renew our fellowship with each other.

In this mutual communion we are reminded that we belong to each other. We are not like the members of a club or lodge, meeting for their weekly activity. We are not bound together by a common interest in religious issues. The bond which unites us is much stronger than that, for we know ourselves to be sharers together in the grace of God, and fellow members in the body of Christ. So we want to express that fellowship. We come not simply to enjoy God's blessing for ourselves but to share it with others.

The Lord's supper is a feast of remembrance. But it is not simply a simultaneous effort by a group of individuals to recall the same event. Rather it is a mutual stimulus. We aim to remind each other of the death of our common Saviour. As we take the bread and wine and as we eat and drink, we are not only stirring our own hearts to remember the Lord's death, we are prompting each other to engage in the same glad recollection.

Such fellowship at the table is also a means of reassurance. Doubts are the special weapon of Satan to undermine the Christian's faith in God. Such doubts come more powerfully when the Christian is on his own. A lonely situation can be the occasion for particular pressure by the devil. To meet with others at the Lord's table is not only to hear afresh the visible word which answers Satan's doubts; it is also to share with each other the reassurance which comes from the word. The God who in wisdom planned the sacrifice of Calvary promises wisdom to His people in all their perplexities. The God whose love gave Christ to die pledges His continuing love to us. The power which raised Him from the dead is the guarantee of our constant strengthening. That wisdom, that love, that power are not simply declared to us as separate believers, but to the worshipping fellowship. At the table we reassure one another as we share together in God's promises.

It is no wonder then that the supper is a joyful occasion. A joy shared is a joy deepened. When we have had some pleasant experience, or enjoyed some special success, it is a natural reaction that we want to share it with others. At a deeper level of spiritual experience we need also to share together. The Greek word for fellowship, *koinonia,* means having things in common. The shared loaf and the shared cup are an outward sign of the inward sharing of hearts.

Some will come to the Lord's table with troubled minds because of some unrelieved anxiety. Some will be there for whom a recent bereavement is still painfully real. Others have hidden disappointments or burdens. But fellowship means not only rejoicing together but weeping together. To share at the table with a mourner is to share in his or her grief. After all we are remembering together the anguish and suffering of a dying Saviour. What better place to share burdens together than at His supper so that even in the midst of the darkness the light of His joy may shine.

There is an added dimension to our fellowship which is often forgotten. We belong to each other, and not only to those in the local congregation, but to the world-wide fellowship of Christians. This means not only a bond with those who share our own standards of affluence — and affluence it is, judged by the grinding poverty of the third world — it means also that we are linked with poor Christians who are not wondering whether they can keep the car or afford a holiday, but whether they and their children can stay alive in face of prevalent hunger. Paul castigated the rich Corinthians who met for the Lord's supper because they ate and drank and ignored the poor and needy in the congregation (1 Cor. 11:17-22). James had similar strictures for those who gave a prominent position to the rich and relegated the poor to a place of lesser importance (James 2:1-13).

It will not, however, be sufficient for us to claim that we do not have such social divisions in our local church — though some of us might be surprised to discover how much latent snobbery there_is! Nor may we clear our own position by pointing to our concern for the sick, the old or the poor in our own congregation. The clamant call of poor and hungry Christians in the third world still sounds in the midst of our comfortable songs. Dare we remain heedless? Can we turn from our communion service to our well-stocked dining tables and our comfortably furnished homes, and forget the cry of the poor? Our giving to famine relief must not simply be an occasional and dutiful response to an emotional appeal. It is rather one practical outworking of our fellowship with others in the body of Christ.

Proclamation

Closely linked to the idea of fellowship is the further truth that we express our fellowship in the mutual proclamation of the death of Christ. 'Whenever you eat this bread and drink this cup, you proclaim the Lord's death' (1 Cor. 11:26). The Greek word Paul uses here for proclaiming is the one used by the girl in Philippi in describing the preaching of the gospel (Acts 16:17). So we at once eliminate any false notion of a eucharistic sacrifice. To show forth the Lord's death is not to display it to God, but to declare it to one another. God declares the visible word to us and we in turn declare that word to each other.

It recalls one feature of the Passover service when the child asked the meaning of the service and the father replied with the familiar recitation of God's deliverance of Israel from Egypt. Of course each Jewish family knew that story well, but it was necessary to hear it declared afresh so that mind and heart should be stirred anew. The story of Calvary is also familiar to Christians, but it is good to hear it declared again and again so that it is kept continually before us. Peter recognizes this necessity of frequent reiteration of familiar truths: 'I will always remind you of these things, even though you know them and are firmly established in the truth you now have. I think it is right to refresh your memory' (2 Peter 1:12-13). Such refreshment comes to us at the table as we echo the word God is speaking to us.

How then do we proclaim Christ's death? Paul makes it plain — it is in eating and drinking. This not only speaks of the death of Christ, but of our reception of the benefits procured for us by His death. We not only take the bread and the cup; we actually eat and drink, and in that physical action we are displaying outwardly the hidden response of our hearts. So our proclamation to one another by our eating and drinking focuses on the death of the Lord, and also on our participation in it, with the consequent enjoyment of the blessings symbolized by the pleasure of a meal. It is a corporate declaration of our total dependence on the grace of God.

Such proclamation is not an inward-looking exercise in mutual encouragement, but rather a prelude to witness to others. We should always be preparing to go out to men and women with the gospel. The Lord's supper is not like a meal in some cosy retreat where we try to get away from the pressures of life. It is much more like a meal in an army canteen near the front line as the troops get ready to go into action. The church militant engages in mutual encouragement before going out again to fight the good fight of faith.

The message we declare to each other at the table also sets the pattern for the word we are to proclaim to men. Our theme, both within the fellowship and out in the market-place, is the same, for we focus on Jesus Christ and Him crucified. As we share the truth together, our hearts are stirred, and with devotion fired we are being prepared to declare to others the message which has set our own being aflame. The passion which lies at the heart of true witness is kindled as the cross which has been at the heart of our communion service is then declared with conviction to men and women in spiritual need of a Saviour.

Repudiation

The oath of allegiance to the emperor which was taken by Roman soldiers was called in Latin *sacramentum.* It was a pledge of unconditional loyalty and at the same time a renunciation of every other allegiance. The word was adopted by Latin-speaking churches and applied to baptism and the Lord's supper, which were viewed as the two sacraments of the gospel. In them the Christian soldier pledged his loyalty to Christ the Lord and at the same time repudiated every other usurping claim.

The note of allegiance and repudiation is seen in baptism with its death to sin and to the world, and its new life of obedience to Christ. It is also seen in the Lord's supper, where acceptance of the terms of the new covenant involves a disavowal of every other loyalty. The confession made at baptism, 'Jesus is Lord,' is the continuing affirmation of the Christian life. Each time we come to the Lord's table we acknowledge our total indebtedness to Christ, and as we say, 'Jesus is Lord,' we give ourselves afresh to Him in unqualified submission. At the same time we turn our backs on anything else which might usurp the place of authority which Christ alone must occupy. Unreserved allegiance to Christ inevitably involves unqualified rejection of every competing claimant.

Paul introduced his discussion of the supper in 1 Corinthians 10 in the context of a warning to flee from idolatry. His argument is that you cannot share in the bread and wine of the communion and at the same time participate in idolatrous worship. You cannot at one and the same time share in the benefits of Christ's death and give some measure of assent to idolatry. The two things are totally incompatible. Jesus must be Lord in an absolute sense and no other lord must hold sway in our lives.

The apostle probes beneath the outer appearance of idolatry. He acknowledges freely that an idol is really nothing at all. It has no life or power. It is a dead product of sinful man. But there is a more sinister factor in the situation since it cloaks an unseen force which lurks in the background. Behind the idols are ranged the demonic powers with Satan as their prince. There lies the continuing rebellion against God. There are the enemies of God's people whom John Bunyan pictured in *The Holy War* attacking the town of Mansoul and trying to hold it against its rightful sovereign King Shaddai and his Prince Emmanuel. Idolatry is one of the devil's potent weapons as he works to turn men and women from submission to the one true and living God. Thus, says Paul, idolaters do not simply bow down to wood and stone. They are ultimately worshipping the dark powers which lie behind the idols. They may be blind to the real significance of what they are doing for it is Satan's great achievement that he darkens the understanding of men. Yet in reality they are in communion with the devil and with his demonic cohorts.

We may tend to think of idolatry as something rather remote, and the subject as a result rather academic. The idols of Greece and Rome seem far away. Even the idols in Hindu temples or the fetishes of primitive tribesmen today may appear to most people to belong to a world far removed from the bustling life of Western Europe. But in fact idolatry is a much wider issue than the adoration of a material image. It is present wherever men give to someone or something the devotion which is due to God alone. Paul speaks of those whose 'god is their stomach' (Phil. 3:19). He describes in Romans 1 an idolatry which made sexual indulgence the goal of life. He castigates covetousness as idolatry (Col. 3:5). In each case the object of a man's affections and ambitions is other than God alone.

It may be difficult for us to think of a glutton or a persistently immoral individual or a man consumed by greed or personal ambition as an idolater. It may be even more difficult for us to think of such people being in communion with the powers of darkness. Yet that is precisely what Paul says is involved. That is why such idolatry is a rejection of the sovereign claims of God and why as a result it is so disastrous for the soul.

Lest we should imagine that any such idolatrous worship, whether crude or sophisticated, is left behind at conversion, it is important to notice the context of Paul's warnings. He is writing to a church of professed believers in Christ, and to those who have exhibited markedly the powerful working of the Holy Spirit. He addresses them as his 'dear friends', and yet he still urges them to 'flee from idolatry'. The Christian is clearly not immune from the blandishments of Satan. Vanity Fair beckons us to partake of the wares provided. Bypath meadow is certainly available for the unwary. Idolatry waits in the shadows ready for any possible welcome to be extended. The need is therefore constantly present that we should repudiate every tendency to idolatry, and that we should do it with determination.

The Lord's supper is one place where the *sacramentum* of allegiance to Christ is pledged, and with it a rejection of every other entangling claim. To share together in the fruit of Christ's passion, to participate in the blessings procured by His death, to feed on the living bread, to drink of the living fountain — all this is irreconcilable with any other dominion. Christ and idols cannot both be enthroned. He must reign supreme, and in our glad acknowledgement at the supper of His sovereign headship, we are at the same time repudiating Satan and every agency he may employ to seduce us.

Abraham followed Jehovah, but this entailed turning his back on Ur of the Chaldees. The law on Mount Sinai forbade the making of graven images, and the ministry of the prophets was a continuing protest against every breach of that clear prohibition. Jesus Himself rejected Satan's advances in the wilderness and refused his request that the Messiah should bow down to him. Each new day and especially each Lord's Day we renew our allegiance. Cowper's hymn furnishes us with a prayer of repudiation:

> The dearest idol I have known,
> Whate'er that idol be,

> Help me to tear it from Thy throne,
> And worship only Thee.

Anticipation

The hope of the second coming of Christ clearly dominated the outlook of the early disciples. The message of the angel just after the ascension had obviously been deeply imprinted on their minds: 'This same Jesus, who has been taken from you into heaven, will come back in the same way you have seen him go into heaven' (Acts 1:11). The fuller knowledge which they received through the gift of the Holy Spirit on the Day of Pentecost, must have shed new light on the parables of Jesus, many of which pointed forward to the return of the Lord and to the consummation of His kingdom. This hope did not detach them from their present duties. On the contrary it gave them a greater incentive since their 'labour in the Lord' was 'not in vain' (1 Cor. 15:58). Nor did suffering or persecution dim their hope since the darkness only made the light of heaven shine more brightly.

The prominence of the story of the exodus as a dominant theme in Christian thinking reminded them of the first Passover in Egypt when the Israelites ate the meal with everything prepared for their journey, and with the Promised Land already in view. The heavenly Canaan is likewise the Christian's prospect, and at each Lord's supper he is pointed to his final goal as he hears the words of the apostle Paul, reminding him that the observance is to be maintained 'until he comes'. The apostle's words were in fact simply an echo of the Lord's own voice. When He met with the disciples in the upper room He was anticipating the heavenly feast to which the Lord's supper is a prelude: 'I have eagerly desired to eat this Passover with you before I suffer. For I tell you, I will not eat it again until it finds fulfilment in the kingdom of God . . . Take this [cup] and divide it among you. For I tell you I will not drink again of the fruit of the vine until the kingdom of God comes' (Luke 22:15-18).

The air of expectancy which is such a marked feature of the New Testament is reflected in the various descriptive titles given to Christians. They are 'aliens' (1 Peter 2:11) even in the land of their birth and although, like many an overseas student, they aim to play their part in the life of the country where they are at present, and while they may indeed greatly appreciate many aspects of its life, yet always their heart is elsewhere. Paul puts it well: 'Our citizenship is in heaven. And we eagerly await a Saviour from there, the Lord Jesus Christ' (Phil. 3:20).

Then again, like the heroes and heroines of faith in Hebrews 11, they are pilgrims on their way to the Celestial City. Abraham, the prototype of the pilgrims, has been joined by a great company who are 'longing for a better country — a heavenly one'. They are confident as they press on for they are persuaded that 'their God . . . has prepared a city for them' (Heb. 11:16). Like Bunyan's pilgrim they may face all the hazards of the way from the Hill Difficulty to Vanity Fair, from the Valley of the Shadow to the Enchanted Ground, but the sight of the Celestial City which they see clearly from the Delectable Mountains summons them so insistently that nothing can hold them back.

They are also soldiers in the army of Prince Emmanuel. They fight against the world, the flesh and the devil, and at times the struggle is severe. Indeed there are seasons when the tide of battle seems to be flowing against them and when they taste the bitter shame of personal defeat. Yet still they prove the mercy of their King and defeat proves to be merely a temporary reverse. They are encouraged by the realization that they belong to the army of the saints, many of whom have already reached the King's presence. An even greater incentive to confident persistence is the knowledge that the King who awaits them has already dealt a crushing blow to every foe, and will finally tread Satan under His feet. So they 'fight the good fight of faith' and keep in view the conqueror's crown.

Furthermore, they are athletes in the arena of faith. Their goal is a greater one than that of the Olympic runners who strove with determination to win the prize. 'They do it', wrote Paul, 'to get a crown that will not last; but we do it to get a crown that will last for ever' (1 Cor. 9:25). It was that unfading glory which still beckoned the apostle in his final days in the condemned cell at Rome as he drew near the end of the race. 'I have fought the good fight, I have finished the race, I have kept the faith. Now there is in store for me the crown of righteousness, which the Lord, the righteous Judge, will award me on that day — and not only to me, but also to all who have longed for his appearing' (2 Tim. 4:7-8). The message of the Epistle to the Hebrews sounds the same note as it calls the Christian athlete to run with persistence. The vision it gives is of the Saviour who is already at the end of the course awaiting each faithful runner. So we 'run with perseverance the race that is set before us, looking to Jesus the pioneer and perfecter of our faith' (Heb. 12:1-2 R.S.V.).

Christians are also described as workmen, or stewards, in the parable of the talents and in that of the pounds. Their responsibility is to be discharged faithfully in view of the Master's return. He Himself tied the call to diligent service with the firm reminder of His own return. Let His disciples therefore always be 'like men waiting for their master. . . . It will be good for those servants whose master finds them watching when he comes. . . . It will be good for those servants whose master finds them ready, even if he comes in the second or third watch of the night. . . . You also must be ready, because the Son of Man will come at an hour when you do not expect him' (Luke 12:35-40).

Such then are Christ's guests who meet at His table. There they meet with their fellow Christians who share the same heavenly citizenship, travel on the same journey, fight the same battles, run the same race, toil in the same service and look forward to the same glorious climax of all their endeavours. They are united also in their great need. They can respond sympathetically to Paul's question: 'Who is equal to such a task?' (2 Cor. 2:16), for they know how utterly inadequate their own resources are. Yet here at His table they are assured of the provision which they need. Endurance for the continuing pilgrimage, courage for the battle, power for the contest, strength for the toil — all are found in the reserves of blessing which are ours in Christ.

Each time we share in the family meal of the people of God we hear the Lord saying, 'My grace is sufficient for you' (2 Cor. 12:9). The promise of God comes to the weary or dispirited or defeated Christian, just as it came through Isaiah to the men of his day. 'Those who hope in the Lord will renew their strength. They will soar on wings like eagles; they will run and not grow weary, they will walk and not be faint' (Isa. 40:31). We do not tread the pilgrim path alone for He says to us, 'Surely I will be with you always' (Matt. 28:20). We do not fight with an uncertainty as to the outcome of the battle, for 'we are more than conquerors through him that loved us' (Rom. 8:37). We do not need to falter in the race, for the Lord who slakes our thirst at His supper will refresh the tired athlete. We can return to the toil with renewed determination having been assured afresh that 'it is God who works in you to will and to act according to his good purpose' (Phil. 2:13).

By keeping the coming of the Lord before us, the Lord's supper not only gives us the incentive to press forward with confidence, but also issues a warning of the dangers of growing slack. It is easy to pay lip-service to the truth that heaven is our home, and at the same time to sink our roots deeply in the soil of this world. We may assent outwardly to the conviction that 'to die is gain' and may welcome in our hymn singing the prospect of the Lord's return, and yet we may be firmly wedded to the affairs of this life. We may indeed be scarcely distinguishable from those around us whose outlook is bounded by purely material considerations. To meet at the Lord's table is to be reminded of our returning Lord, and at the same time to be warned of the dangers of settling down in a complacent and comfortable worldliness.

The Lord's supper is not a form of escapism. It is not an attempt to opt out of the situation and to forget about the issues which confront us in the world outside. The pilgrim in the 'House Beautiful', the soldier on the reserve lines, the athlete during a brief respite from vigorous training, the workman in his meal break — all are preparing for their return to the tasks ahead. The Christian at the Lord's table has withdrawn for the moment from the everyday demands of life, but it is with a view to returning refreshed to face them. However, beyond those tasks and beyond the faithful discharge of his responsibilities he glimpses the coming glory when the Lord, whom he sees by faith presiding at the table, will be seen in the full splendour of His heavenly reign. E. H. Bickersteth's communion hymn keeps that vision before us, as we look back to the cross and look forward to the crown:

> See the feast of love is spread!
> Drink the wine and break the bread —

Sweet memorials — till the Lord
Call us round His heavenly board;
Some from earth, from glory some,
Severed only 'till He come'.

Self-examination

The apostle's teaching on the Lord's supper begins with a
word of rebuke to the Corinthians, and ends with a solemn
reminder of the importance of preparation of heart, and of
a right attitude in coming to the Lord's table. The word of
censure was due to their having treated the Lord's supper as
if it were like any other meal. They had behaved as if they
were simply men and women gathered for a social occasion,
rather than fellow members of the body of Christ summoned
by the Lord for fellowship with the Saviour and with each
other. The sad consequence had been the unhappy divisions
which reflected the factional spirit at Corinth, and which led
to a selfish unconcern for fellow believers. Instead of unity
which produces a sensitive concern for the needs of others,
there was division which led to criticism, backbiting, gossip
and all the ugly symptoms of a self-centred attitude.

Paul's reply to this sorry situation is a strong reminder of
the purpose for which the Lord instituted the supper. It is
the visible word which declares the grace and mercy of God
to sinners, and so it puts every guest at the table on the same
level of need. Social, economic, racial and all other distinc-
tions fade into insignificance in the face of their common
indebtedness to the pardoning grace of God. Here is the place
where forgiven sinners meet together to praise their common
Saviour, and to proclaim to one another the wonder of His
death on their behalf. It was against this background of the
Lord's aim in the observance of the supper and their sad
failure to realize that aim that the apostle stressed the seriousness of unworthy communion and the need for sober self-
assessment in coming to share in the Lord's supper.

To speak of unworthy participation is to face the possibility
that some very scrupulous Christian may interpret this in
such a way that he feels excluded from the table. Knowing
his own heart, and his inconsistencies and failures, he may

feel that he is not worthy to come to the Lord's table. Yet surely such a realization of unfitness, far from being a barrier, is in fact the basic qualification for coming. To acknowledge our sins before God does not result in the divine enforcement of an exclusion order. Rather it leads to God's gracious promises of forgiveness and cleansing through the blood of Christ. It is not the penitent believer, who feels so deeply his need of the mercy of God, who is guilty of unworthy participation, for to him the supper is a gracious pledge of God's welcoming grace. It is rather the complacency and dullness of conscience which leads to participation without preparation of heart, and without repentance and faith, which are the subject of Paul's solemn warning.

It is not sin which makes us unfit, for there is a ready pardon for penitent sinners. It is clinging to our sins which sets up a barrier which we cross at our peril. It is not David lamenting his sin in Psalm 51 who is excluded from God's presence, but David during the months when he refused to confess. In Psalm 32 he recalls his persistent refusal to acknowledge his grievous fault, with the consequent dryness of soul: 'When I kept silent, my bones wasted away through my groaning all day long' (Ps. 32:3). It was only when he came to the point of definite repentance that pardon came: 'I said, "I will confess my transgressions to the Lord" — and you forgave the guilt of my sin' (Ps. 32:5). Both psalms enlarge on the exuberance of spirit which followed his repentance, and which led him to a renewed sharing in worship. Elsewhere he formulates the same principle: 'If I had cherished sin in my heart, the Lord would not have listened' (Ps. 66:18). To approach God with unconfessed sin and an impenitent heart is to be rejected. To come with grief of spirit and with shame at sinful failure is to find an overflowing pardon and a gracious welcome.

A further reason for unworthy communion is unresolved divisions among Christians. This was a major cause of Paul's censure of the Corinthians, but it is still only too frequently the same issue which mars, and indeed destroys, what should be a rich experience. The Lord Jesus dealt with this matter when He spoke of the qualification for going to the altar in the temple, and the same applies to those who would come to the Lord's table: 'Therefore, if you are offering your gift at the altar and there remember that your brother has something against you, leave the gift there in front of the altar. First go and be reconciled to your brother; then come and offer your gift' (Matt. 5:23-24). He taught the same lesson when he gave them the pattern prayer: 'Forgive us our debts, as we also have forgiven our debtors.' He reinforced the point by the additional warning: 'If you do not forgive men their sins, your Father will not forgive your sins' (Matt. 6:15). In His parable He spoke of the unforgiving servant who had been relieved by his master of a huge debt and yet would not make any concession to one who owed him a paltry sum. For such a servant there was only judgement, and for a Christian who has an unforgiving spirit there is the same censure. Let him not presume to come to the Lord's table until he has put things right.

But what if the other Christian refuses to be reconciled? If you have apologized for whatever you said or did which was a genuine cause of offence, and if you have offered to make amends, and if, in spite of all your efforts, you still meet a blank wall, what then? The answer to that question is in the Lord's own instructions in Matthew 18:15-18 where a determined attempt is to be made to resolve the difference — in this case it is the aggrieved one who takes the initiative, but the principle remains the same. Every effort is to be made to heal the breach. If, however, one party refuses to receive either the personal approach or that of two or three witnesses, or even of the church, then he is to be excluded from the fellowship; but the man who has aimed at reconciliation is free to join in corporate worship with his fellow believers.

The self-centred attitude seen in Corinth led then, and still leads, to a lack of concern and respect for others, and this is a further bar to communion. To ignore a fellow Christian is bad enough, but to despise a fellow Christian is even worse. To look down on others because of their social status or their lack of abilities, as the critic sees them, is a grievous sin. Such sin if it is not confessed to the Lord brings judgement. There is no room for snobs at the Lord's table, whether that snobbery is social, intellectual, racial or religious. The only people who are welcome are those who are glad to accept all who can share in the same humbling confession: 'By the grace of God I am what I am.'

How strongly Paul puts the case against unworthy communion! He presents it as a crime against the Lord: 'Whoever eats the bread or drinks the cup of the Lord in an unworthy manner will be guilty of sinning against the body and blood of the Lord' (1 Cor. 11:27). It is a very serious indictment, and yet it inevitably follows from his teaching on the nature of the supper. Since the bread and wine are the divinely appointed means of declaring to us the body and blood of Christ given for us, then to take these outward signs with unconfessed sin in our hearts or bitterness of spirit or contempt of others — this is to insult the Lord. It is to join the ranks of those who not only crucified the Lord but mocked Him in His dying hours. Such a crime is so serious that the very possibility of committing it should sober the Christian into a realization of his great need to be truly prepared for the Lord's table.

There is, however, a further word of warning. The unworthy participant 'eats and drinks judgement on himself' (1 Cor. 11:29). The rendering in the Authorized Version, 'damnation', suggests eternal condemnation, but clearly this is not in view since, in verse 32, Paul contrasts the judgement of the Lord, which is His way of disciplining believers, and the condemnation of the world. It is, of course, true that the unregenerate person who comes to the Lord's table in a continuing state of unbelief aggravates his guilt and hastens his condemnation. For such a one the word 'damnation' would fit his condition. Yet at the same time we must not minimize the seriousness of the warning to the Christian, and the severity of the judgement of the Lord on His own people. They may rejoice that 'there is no condemnation for those who are in Christ Jesus' and yet they may still dread the possibility of the Lord's grave censure.

When God's people refuse to accept His rebuke they will be compelled to face His chastening. So David faced the consequences not only of his adultery, but of his impenitence, and the child born out of the illicit relationship died. Ananias and Sapphira were struck down by God and great fear came on the church. Here at Corinth there was sickness and death, which Paul sees as evidence of divine judgement. We must not, of course, draw the totally false conclusion that all sickness is a sign of the judgement of God. The book of Job and the Lord's rejection of such a notion in the case of the man born blind should disabuse us of such a false idea. Yet at the same time we must reckon on the severity of God's chastening whether in our bodies, our businesses, our homes or in the miscarriage of our plans. We need the 'great fear' which was one feature of the church in the Acts of the Apostles. There was no incompatibility between that great fear and their great joy. Chastening after all is not intended solely as a penalty but as a sharp instrument to humble us and to impel us to turn to the Lord for forgiveness.

In view of the serious consequences of unworthy communion there is clearly a continuing need for rigorous self-examination. Obviously this is not to be perverted into morbid introspection which does not strengthen us but drives us in on ourselves with paralysing effects. Healthy self-examination is, however, a necessity and perhaps more especially at the present time, when a superficial evangelicalism so readily peddles security and dismisses any self-scrutiny as if it was a token of a lack of faith. The call to 'examine yourselves . . . test yourselves' (2 Cor. 13:5) is one which we dare not ignore.

We should notice that in this exercise we are called to be actively engaged. It is true that we must submit to the Lord's scrutiny and indeed should pray in the words of the psalmist: 'Search me, O God, and know my heart' (Ps. 139:23). At the same time Paul speaks here of the Christian engaging in the task of self-examination himself.

Examinations imply standards. Students face tests in order to discover if they have reached the required academic level in their subject, and it is in relation to that criterion that either a pass or fail is registered. The Christian also has a standard by which to assess himself. It is the law of God! So he turns afresh to the Ten Commandments, to the summary of those commandments, to Jesus' detailed exposition of the law in the sermon on the mount, and to the perfect embodiment of the law in Jesus' own life. He turns to the practical and searching requirements of the Epistles, and to the illustrations furnished by the record of the early believers in the Acts. So he asks: 'Do I love God with all my heart and my neighbour as myself? Do I tolerate idols in my life? Do I take the Lord's name in an empty way for formal prayer and false professions of spiritual achievement? Do I treat the Lord's

Day as one of spiritual drudgery or one of glad worship? Do I conceal hatred, which in Jesus' words is as bad as murder? Do I cling to adulterous thoughts? Do I steal another's reputation by my gossip or covet his position or his gifts by my envy?'

Clearly such self-examination is not content with a survey of our outward actions. The external righteousness of the Pharisee is not the standard for the Christian. So he must probe below the surface into his thought life where festering bitterness or self-assertive ambition can be dominant. He must open up the picture-gallery of his imagination where uncleanness may be tolerated. He must examine the motives which lie behind his actions and which can rob what seems good in the sight of men of any worth in the sight of God. Above all he must be alert to detect any evidence of the corrupting effects of pride, that fundamental abomination of sinful men and women.

Self-examination is not, however, an end in itself. To engage in it without turning to the Lord is only to end in despair. The aim rather is that it should lead us to a frank confession of our sins to the Lord. The shame of soul which comes when we realize how much hidden iniquity lurks within us should lead us to the fountain opened for sin and uncleanness in the blood of Christ. The grief of spirit which accompanies self-examination is intended to be only a prelude to the renewed joy of forgiveness. It is in the assurance of that forgiveness that we may come to the Lord's table with confidence.

If there has been a breach of fellowship with another Christian, or if we have injured someone, whether Christian or unbeliever, by our own sinful words or deeds, then it is not enough to confess our sins to the Lord, we must make things right with those we have hurt. Care, however, is needed here. If the injury or the adultery or the theft have not gone beyond the bounds of our own thoughts, then clearly it is to the Lord alone we should confess. To go to someone with a confession of impure desires of which they were totally ignorant would only be a source of embarrassment or even temptation to that person. When the sin is known only to God and ourselves then to God alone we must confess it. When it has involved another either by omission or commission then we have the further responsibility of confessing to them.

There is one way of meeting an awareness of sinful failure which is not available to us. It is to abstain from attendance at the Lord's table. Certainly we should not come if we know ourselves to be unfit. But to try to avoid coming to terms with our spiritual failure by opting out of communion is only to compound our guilt by a rejection of the Lord's invitation to His table. Paul has no intention of keeping people away from the Lord's table. He wants them to come, but to come in the right way, as penitent sinners seeking and finding forgiveness in Christ. There is no place for a Judas, no place for a self-righteous Pharisee, no place for a gospel hypocrite. But for the Christian who has sinned, but grieves deeply over his sin, there is a place. Indeed there is more than a place, there is a warm invitation and a ready welcome. What better place for forgiven sinners than the table where the Lord presides, and in the broken bread and outpoured wine declares to His assembled guests: 'Though your sins are like scarlet, they shall be as white as snow; though they are red like crimson, they shall be like wool'? (Isa. 1:18.)

11 Amen!

Usage certainly varies. There is the sonorous 'Amen' from the pulpit to which the response is total silence. There is the elaborate musical 'Amen' which in some congregations is considered to be the appropriate finale to the service. There is a congregational response which ranges from a perfunctory mumble to a virtually non-stop background sound. For some it seems to be a kind of liturgical semi-colon or full stop indicating either the ending of one item of worship or the final closure of the service. For some it appears to be some form of emotional release; for others a routine formula to be repeated at traditional intervals — the local tradition dictating how long or short those intervals should be. Mercifully there are also many for whom a fervent 'Amen' is clearly an expression of confident faith and of glad worship.

Turning to the Bible, we find the word 'Amen' used extensively in both the Old and New Testaments, and particularly by the Lord Jesus Christ. It comes from a Hebrew word whose root meaning is 'to strengthen'. Hence it is used as a word of confirmation by which a statement is firmly underscored by the speaker, or complete acceptance is indicated by the hearer. In either case the one who says, 'Amen,' lends his personal weight to what is said, whether by stressing that he means what he says, or by assuring others that he welcomes and concurs with the statement which has been made.

Christ's very frequent use of the word is obscured for English readers by the Authorized Version which translates it 'verily'. It is, however, His regular word for emphasizing His message, and especially an issue of particular significance. His 'Amen' thus precedes many of His claims, His commands and His promises. This element of emphasis is brought out even more forcibly in John's Gospel where the 'Amen, Amen, I say to you' with its duplicated refrain adds a further dimension of emphasis.

It is as if the Lord were saying, 'This is of signal importance and particular significance to you. So I want you to pay especial heed to it and that is why why I am emphasizing it.' So the 'Amen' of the Lord Jesus is His assurance that we may take His word seriously and rely on it with implicit confidence.

This same truth is reflected in Paul's emphatic words to the Corinthians (2 Cor. 1:20) where all the promises of God are reinforced by the emphatic 'Yes' of Christ. If we follow Calvin and most of the commentators, the 'Amen' which follows is the response of the believers to these promises. But this brings into focus the fact that our 'Amen' is simply an echo of Christ's 'Yes'; and in speaking his decisive 'Yes' to the promises he is continuing the 'Amen, Amen, I say to you' of John's Gospel.

John's vision on Patmos of the ascended and glorified Lord has the same message. Each of the letters to the seven churches comes with the solemn authentication of the authority of the Lord. In the message to Laodicea (Rev. 3:14) He not only speaks 'the Amen' which corroborates the promises but is Himself personally 'the Amen'. His present exaltation, as the One whose work has been finished and whose sacrifice has been accepted, is the pledge that the promises of God will be fully honoured. Having been designated Lord, and given all authority in heaven and on earth, He embodies in His own person the emphatic 'Amen' of God that no word of promise will fail.

It is with the background of the Lord's use of 'Amen' that its widespread employment in Scripture by the Lord's people can be appreciated. Their 'Amen' is their response to His. This is, of course, the basic pattern of Scripture. God at every point has taken the initiative both in creation and redemption. He has taken the first step in revealing Himself to men. He has spoken, both in His mighty deeds and in the commentary on those deeds which He Himself has given. The answering response to the divine initiative is faith, and faith utters its grateful 'Amen' to all that God has said and done.

Thus we find the word used in the first place as assent to the declaration of the Word of God. When Moses proclaimed the curses of God which were to be read on Mount Ebal after their entry into Canaan the prescribed word of assent to each individual sentence of judgement on specific acts of disobedience was to be a united 'Amen' spoken by all the people. There is an echo of that response in the reply of the people to the call of Nehemiah. Again it was a word of judgement coupled with a summons to repentance. The people in acknowledgement of their sinful failure pledged obedience; and as a token of their fidelity to the pledge they unitedly joined in the 'Amen' which, because it was an open response to the Word of God, issued in praise.

The book of Revelation (1:7; 22:20,21) has the same pattern of assent to the Word finding expression in a spoken response. The recurring promise in the Apocalypse is the personal and triumphant return of Christ. So in the opening chapter John appends his own 'Amen' to his declaration of the coming of the Lord, and in the closing chapter he replies in the same way. The glorified Lord leaves His last word with His church: 'Surely I am coming soon.' John's Spirit-taught reply is the continuing response of the church, in which assent moves into prayer: 'Amen. Come, Lord Jesus.'

The usage of 'Amen' in prayer and praise is a characteristic feature of the worshipping church, and it is rooted in biblical practice. In 1 Corinthians 14 when Paul is discussing the issue of speaking in a tongue in the congregational gathering, he insists that either an interpretation must be given or the speaker must be silent. His argument is that the congregation must be able to participate in the prayer which is being offered. So he puts the issue firmly — how can the man who does not know the tongue say 'the Amen' at the giving of thanks? Clearly Paul envisages the utterance of this 'Amen' as being the normal practice of the church. It is the believers' affirmation before God that they are united in spirit with the one who is leading them in prayer. It is no mere mechanical or routine performance for it involves an intelligent grasp of what is being said.

Benedictions in the New Testament are really forms of prayer. To pronounce a blessing on an individual or a church is an implicit prayer that God would bless them. This explains why the blessings of Romans 15:33: 'The God of peace be with you all', and that of Galatians 6:18: 'The grace of our Lord Jesus Christ be with your spirit, brothers', are both followed by the customary endorsement: 'Amen'. Paul's personal greeting in 1 Corinthians 16:24: 'My love be with you all in Christ Jesus', is so close to a benediction that it obviously seemed appropriate that he should round it off with his own 'Amen'.

It is in the realm of praise that the Amen rings out so powerfully and so frequently both in the Old Testament and in the New. Believers cannot listen to praise being offered to God and remain dumb. They are not spectators watching someone else perform, nor hearers listening to another's words. Such is their own grateful response to the glory of God that they must participate. The praise which one believer offers is theirs as well, and their fervent 'Amen' is their own glad affirmation of their indebtedness to the grace of God. When David appoints the psalm of thanksgiving to be sung to the Lord by Asaph and his brethren the final burst of praise is answered by the 'Amen'. It is not only Asaph and his brethren who offer praise, but those who join with them in worship. But it is no silent assent, for 'all the people said "Amen" and "Praise the Lord"' (1 Chron. 16:36).

The Psalter is supremely the praise manual of the Old Testament, and here again and again the 'Amen' rings out. Particularly noticeable is the usage in Psalms 41:13; 72:19 and 89:52 where the response is duplicated. It is as if the majesty and glory of God so overwhelm the psalmist that he cannot content himself with a single ending to the psalm, but must overflow in the repeated finale, 'Amen and Amen'. There were doubtless those in the Old Testament church who were as sluggish in spirit as we often are. But David leaves no room for a silent congregation giving a muted assent. Praise must come from all the people, so, 'Let all the people say, "Amen!"' (Ps. 106:48.)

The New Testament writers, steeped as they were in the Psalms, naturally reflect the same pattern of praise. When Paul in Romans 11:36 pens his great paean of praise to the sovereign God who is the source, the sustainer and goal of all things, he adds to his ascription of praise his heartfelt 'Amen'. He repeats it in Ephesians 3:21 when he ascribes glory to the God 'who is able to do immeasurably more than all we ask or imagine'. In the closing verses of the Epistle to the Hebrews the 'Amen' is repeated twice after both the doxology and the benediction. The praise of the Apocalypse (Rev. 1:6; 19:4) receives the same joyful endorsement from the apostle on Patmos and from the congregation in heaven as they utter their 'Amen'. In the latter case it is fittingly coupled with its appropriate companion, 'Hallelujah'.

The God of Scripture is the faithful God. He comes to His people in grace and makes His promises with an abundant liberality. Nor does He leave any room for doubt. He means what He says and will perform every word. Christ is His pledge and the Son's 'Amen' is the declaration of the Father's faithfulness. To such reiterated promises from heaven the response of the believer is a humble and grateful acknowledgement of the goodness of God, prayer for the fulfilling of God's purposes, and praise that God is able to exceed in bounty all that we may ask. Whether in such acknowledgement of God's goodness, whether in prayer or in praise, the characteristic response to the gracious 'Amen' of heaven is the glad and adoring 'Amen' of the church.

Jerome in the fourth century described the worship of the church of his day. The 'Amen' of the congregation sounded, he said, like thunder. He would hardly write like that of many of our congregations today, where a barely perceptible whisper, or at best a slight murmur, is the most that people seem able to muster. How can we sing the Psalms of David, or how can we read the ascriptions of praise in the New Testament without being moved? But to be moved deeply is to look for a means of expression. The biblical expression is, however, ready for use. Let David himself emphasize the point: 'Let all the people say, "Amen".' Let Nehemiah describe the uninhibited response to such a summons to praise: 'And all the people answered, "Amen, Amen".' Let Jude touch our lips with the fire of the Spirit as he reaches his final crescendo of praise: 'To him who is able to keep you from falling and to present you before his glorious presence without fault and with great joy — to the only God our Saviour be glory, majesty, power and authority, through Jesus Christ our Lord, before all ages, now and evermore! Amen.'

12 Hallelujah!

A certain measure of inconsistency in the main English versions of the Bible obscures the fact that the word 'Hallelujah' occurs much more frequently in the Psalms than might appear in a public reading. The translators adopted a different policy when translating the Psalms from that employed in their rendering of the book of Revelation. In the former case they actually translated the word 'Hallelujah' as 'Praise the Lord', while indicating in the margin the original Hebrew word.

In the case of the four occurrences of the word in Revelation 19 they simply transposed the Greek word into English letters to give the word 'Hallelujah'. In the latter case they followed the line taken by the translators of the Old Testament Septuagint Greek version, who transliterated the Hebrew word into a Greek form 'Allelouia' — the word which in turn was used by the apostle John in the song of praise in Revelation 19.

While it was quite correct to translate the word in the Psalms, it did obscure the difference between 'Hallelujah' and the phrase usually translated in the same way. The difference is that in the case of the word 'Hallelujah' it is the shorter version of the divine name which is used — rendered by the Authorized Version (Ps. 68:4) as Jah. In the other occurrences it is the full name of the Lord which is employed. In both cases the common feature is the verb *Hallal* which means to praise. The distinction suggests that the term 'Hallelujah' was in fact a special cry or ejaculation of praise used in worship.

The word appears twenty-four times in the Psalms as a summons to praise. Sometimes it comes at the end of a psalm (Pss 104; 105; 115; 116; 117), sometimes at the beginning (111; 112) and sometimes both at the beginning and the end (106; 113; 135; 146 — 150). In one place only it appears within the psalm (135:3) but in this case it may be seen as a resumption, after a short introduction, of the initial 'Hallelujah' in the same psalm.

This variation in usage suggests that the word was used as an introductory summons to praise, and also as a climax of the praise already offered. This note of climax is particularly evident in Psalm 106:48 where it is linked with 'Amen' to provide a twofold response of praise following the recital of God's gracious and powerful deeds on behalf of his people. This conjunction of 'Amen' and 'Hallelujah' is reflected in Nehemiah 5:13 where 'The whole assembly said, "Amen," and praised the Lord.' The same twofold response is seen in Revelation 19:4 where the final 'Hallelujah' is preceded by 'Amen'.

Whether it is heard as a call to a congregation to praise God, or as the joyful response of those who are exulting in God's grace and mercy, the word focuses mind and heart and voice on God Himself. He is not only the object of our praise but is also the reason for it. We not only praise God, but we do so because He is the Lord who is worthy to be praised. It is because He is the kind of God Scripture has declared Him to be, and because the people of God down the years have proved Him to be all that Scripture reveals, that we join with our fellow members of the church of God in our hallelujah chorus.

The divine name which, as we have seen, is a constituent element in the word, reminds us that God is the Lord who has revealed Himself. This name by which He made Himself known was revealed in order to declare His character and His purposes to His people. For that reason the name of the Lord is quite distinct from the names which paganism or the great ethnic religions have produced to designate their deities. Such names represent human attempts to convey the idea that the worshipper has in mind as he approaches his god. The divine name in the Old Testament, however, is of a totally different character. It is not the product of men's religious reflections but is rather the name by which God Himself designated His uniqueness and revealed His nature to men. The name of the Lord is not an echo of men's thoughts but is in fact a statement made by God Himself.

Implied in this name is the underlying idea of eternity.

God is the great 'I am' who is without beginning or end. He did not come into existence at some point of time in the remote past. His origin cannot be fixed as a historical fact like the origin of the created order. He is from everlasting to everlasting. He is the eternal God. He knows neither change nor decay. He is not trapped in the constant ebb and flow of time. He is bound neither by the clock nor by the calendar. He has not emerged from the past with a personal record of growth and development; nor is He moving tentatively towards an uncertain future. He is, rather, the ever-present one for whom the unfolding pattern of history is always 'now'. Every time then that the Spirit of God elicits from us the cry, 'Hallelujah!' He is reminding us that we worship the eternal God. Our praise is not a song which will be snuffed out in the chill silence of death but will resound with perennial freshness for ever and ever.

The eternal God is the Creator of all things. This is the basic truth with which the Bible begins. It is the truth which again and again so thrills the writers of the Psalms that they burst out in praise. To contemplate the glory of the heavens, the wonder of the seasons, the flocks and herds with their young, the fields with their maturing harvest, the vineyards with their abounding fruit — to contemplate these and innumerable other manifestations of the marvels of nature is to feel one's heart lifted to the God who made it all. It is no wonder that the Psalms end in a final call to every living creature: 'Let every thing that has breath praise the Lord. Hallelujah' (150:6).

The Lord of creation in the Old Testament is also 'the Lord of hosts'. He is the God of the nations. He is not like the localized deities of the pagan world with their limited domain and their petty interests. He is the Lord of all the nations. He is the God of history, who by His sovereign providence directs and controls all events to achieve His ultimate purpose of glorifying His own name. It is this sense of history, with its accompanying awareness of the sovereignty of God Almighty, which makes our 'Hallelujah', not the muted refrain of a rather uncertain minority movement, but the joyful acclaim of those who are supremely confident of the final triumph of the Lord.

When the Lord revealed His name to Moses it was in the

context of His commission to go and lead Israel out of Egypt. The Lord is the Redeemer who sets His people free. That national deliverance was prophetic. It pointed to the greater deliverance accomplished by Christ whose victory at Calvary has redeemed His people from the dominion of sin. The theme of redemption continues throughout the Scripture and the response is constantly one of praise and thanksgiving. Redemption implies the grace and mercy of God who does not deal in judgement with men as their rebellion fully warrants, but freely forgives them and emancipates them from their spiritual slavery. It is no surprise therefore to hear those who are described as 'the redeemed of the Lord' responding in praise. That praise reaches its climax in the Apocalypse of John where redemption is still the dominant note: 'To him who loves us and has freed us from our sins by his blood, and has made us to be a kingdom and priests to serve his God and Father — to him be glory and power for ever and ever! Amen' (Rev. 1:5-6).

Our Creator and Redeemer has also revealed Himself as the God of the covenant. His name declares His gracious establishment of a personal relationship with men and women whom He has freely pardoned and whom He has brought into fellowship with Himself. He says to these former rebels, 'You are my people.' With gratitude they reply, 'You are our God.' It is this deep sense of indebtedness to God's mercy, this overwhelming awareness of His gracious pardon, this humbling realization of the privilege of being the people of God — it is all these which move us to a burst of praise for which the word 'Hallelujah' provides the most succinct, and at the same time the most complete response.

The various aspects of God's nature and of His merciful dealings with His people are summarized in the song of praise in Revelation 19. It is because 'salvation and glory and power belong to our God' (19:1) that the great throng of worshippers bursts into song. He is the God who saves sinners with an everlasting salvation. He is the God whose truth has blazed out in a world of darkness to display His glory in His mighty works of creation, providence and redemption. He is the God of power whose might is seen in the record of creation, in His judgement of the nations, in the great miracles of the Incarnation and the resurrection of Christ, and which will be seen finally in the coming again of the Saviour. Such salvation, glory and power, can only elicit an exultant response and so, again and again, the multitude cry out, 'Hallelujah!'

The praise of the Psalms and the songs of the Apocalypse both build up towards a climax. The Psalter ends with a crescendo of instrumental music and song which reach their triumphant finale in the last psalm. Every instrument is summoned to contribute to the great symphony. Every mortal tongue is commanded to yield its measure of praise. So, with the clash of the cymbals and the swelling notes of the trumpets, the climactic burst of praise from all creation rises to the final glorious 'Hallelujah'.

In Revelation 19 there is the same pattern. John heard 'what sounded like the roar of a great multitude in heaven'. They shout their triumphant 'Hallelujah!' They are borne forward by the exaltation of spirit which springs from a realization that the final judgements of the Almighty have come. 'Again they shouted: "Hallelujah!"'. The twenty-four elders and the four beasts — a symbol perhaps of the complete people of God from the twelve tribes and from the apostolic church, and also of the whole created order — these also join in the victorious acclaim as they fall down and worship before the throne and cry, 'Amen, Hallelujah!'

Then comes the final shout of victory. It sounds to John in his lonely exile in a Roman penal colony 'like a great multitude' shouting praise to their God. 'Like the roar of rising water' the praise floods on in a torrent of music and song. There is no ebb in the surging waves of praise, no lull in the swelling notes of joy. Then it reaches new heights as 'like loud peals of thunder' the song of innumerable saints moves towards a climax. It is the consummation of the songs of the suffering church in every generation, the hymns of the pilgrim church in every century of advance or decline, the thanksgiving of a great host of forgiven sinners drawn from every tribe and nation and tongue. Every joyful note blends with the triumph song of heaven. It is the climax of the everlasting purposes of God. The eternal day has dawned and night will never come again. Sin is forever banished and with it all the discordant ugliness of sickness, sorrow and death. Now is the final authentication of the gospel, and now also the supreme vindication of Christ Jesus the Lord. Heaven is alive with song as the music moves to a crescendo of praise. The worship of the triumphant church rises to a glorious finale: 'Hallelujah! For our Lord God Almighty reigns.'